MEXICANA!

ESTHER CLARK

MEXICANA!

FOR THE LOVE OF TACOS, NACHOS AND ALL THINGS FIESTA

HarperCollins*Publishers*

CONTENTS

INTRODUCTION 6

TACOS 14

NACHOS 40

SNACKS 68

SALSAS AND PICKLES 92

SWEET THINGS 108

DRINKS 122

INDEX 138

ACKNOWLEDGEMENTS 143

INTRODUCTION

It's fair to say that, until recently, thoughts of Mexican food tended to conjure up a bowl of salty shop-bought tortilla chips piled up with a few under-seasoned, mediocre toppings, or a slightly sad, soggy takeaway burrito. But help is at hand! In the following pages, such uninspiring stereotypes are turned on their head. Out with the bland and stodgy and in with vibrant, spicy flavours and delicious fresh textures: soft homemade tacos filled with slow-cooked marinated pork shoulder or crispy squid and chipotle aioli (pages 36 and 30); jugs of margarita spiked with seasonal fruit flavours (pages 124–127); and thick wedges of sweet tres leches cake topped with boozy coconut rum cream (page 114).

Mexicana is ideal for sharing. So, seat yourself comfortably, push up your sleeves and get stuck in: salsas for dipping into, nachos for pulling apart and tacos to fill and roll up in a delicious bundle. There is a time and a place for meticulously planned dinner parties, with individual courses served one after another. But this isn't it! When you're feeling a little more casual, there's something to be said for piling food into bowls and onto big sharing platters, laying the table with a funky cloth, filling glasses with ice-cold margaritas, passing round the napkins and digging in while catching up with friends and family. There are no rules for how to serve these dishes, so you can mix and match to suit everyone's taste. Invite friends round after a drink at the pub for a shared feast; dig into Breakfast Tacos (page 18) with your housemates after a heavy night out; or simply share a bowl of nachos with your partner on a cosy Saturday evening in. In *Mexicana!* there are recipes for the Mexican purist and twists on more traditional dishes but, either way, these colourful, well-balanced recipes, packed with delicious ingredients, are here to ignite your inner fiesta!

WHAT TO KEEP IN YOUR STORE CUPBOARD

When venturing into Mexicana a number of ingredients are essential for creating those iconic Mexican flavours. Some are easily obtainable from major supermarkets such as Waitrose or Sainsbury's. Others may require a little more digging to track them down. Online stores such as Sous Chef, Mexgrocer and Amazon stock a wide range of exciting Mexican produce.

KEY MEXICAN DRIED CHILLIES

The chilli pepper lies at the heart of many a Mexican dish. Dried Mexican chillies each have their own distinctive character, with varying levels of heat, and each works well in different dishes. Here are a few examples of some good chillies to keep stored in jars in your pantry or kitchen cupboard.

ANCHO:

The ancho is large, dark and prune-like in appearance. Mild heat-wise, with fruity yet bitter notes, it works well in tomato-based dishes.

CHILE DE ÁRBOL:

Long and spindly in appearance, this chilli is grassy in flavour and medium in heat. Try sprinkled on top of a rich Mexican Hot Chocolate (page 136) or rehydrated in boiling water and stirred through a stew.

CHIPOTLE:

Essentially a fresh jalapeño that has been smoked and dried. Chipotles are deep red in colour and rich and intensely smoky in flavour and aroma. Perfect with dark meat and in salsas. A good staple dried chilli to have in your store cupboard.

HABANERO:

The fieriest of Mexican chillies grown in Latin America, with a shrivelled exterior and fruity yet deeply peppery scent. Be sparing with these fire crackers and rehydrate in boiling water before using. It's best to use latex gloves when handling them – and avoid all contact with the eyes!

STORE-CUPBOARD ESSENTIALS

AGAVE NECTAR/SYRUP:

A natural sweetener in liquid form. Use to add sweetness when mixing margaritas (pages 124–127).

AVOCADO OIL:

A yellowish-green oil, rich in flavour, this is usually to be found with olive oil at your local supermarket. It is lovely drizzled on guacamole (page 102) or whisked into dressings.

CANNED BLACK BEANS:

Easy to find at your local corner shop, black beans play a key role in many Mexican recipes. Simply stir into a dish at the end or mash with olive oil and dollop on nachos (page 44).

CANNED REFRIED BEANS:

Creamy smashed beans such as pinto or black beans. Buy the best-quality varieties as it makes all the difference. Trying adding them to a crisp torta (a Mexican toasted sandwich – page 78).

CANNED TOMATILLOS:

Green fruits that look similar to tomatoes but are smaller in size. You can buy cans of these online. Try whizzing them into a moreish bowl of Green Tomatillo Salsa (page 98).

CHILLI FLAKES:

Always have a jar of these knocking around in your cupboard. Dark, speckled chipotle chilli flakes are perfect for adding that barbecue flavour to dishes. Mash into softened butter and spread on griddled corn on the cob or charred steak.

CHILLI POWDER:

Finely ground chilli powder, in different strengths, is a key addition to your spice shelf. Try chilli powders based on specific varieties of chilli, such as ancho or de árbol, to vary the flavour.

CHIPOTLE CHILLI PASTE:

A nifty small jar of rich, intense chilli paste made with chipotle peppers. Easy to get hold of from most supermarkets and perfect swirled through many dishes.

CHIPOTLES IN ADOBO:

A small can of chipotles in adobo can pep up even the blandest of dishes. Plump chipotle chillies are soaked in a rich tomato sauce with a vinegary aftertaste. Try blitzing them and stirring through aioli (page 107) or adding to homemade ketchup.

CHOLULA CHILLI SAUCE:

A zingy Mexican condiment made with de árbol and piquin peppers. Not too hot, it's delicious splashed onto tacos before serving.

CORNMEAL/POLENTA:

Coarse flour made from dried maize. Use it to sprinkle on empanadas (page 80) or to make moist cornbread (page 88). You'll find this in the world-food section of your supermarket, usually with the Caribbean food.

DRIED HIBISCUS FLOWERS:

Dark pink dried blooms, a bit like curled-up small sea creatures in appearance, these are hugely popular in Mexico. The flowers aren't actually eaten, but soaked in boiling water to make a fruity tea (page 131). Hibiscus has a rich berry flavour, not unlike blackcurrant or cranberry. Delicious for flavouring ice lollies (popsicles) (page 118).

MASA HARINA FLOUR:

A fine, gluten-free flour for making your own tacos from scratch (page 16). With a short shelf life, the flour, made from corn (maize), is best kept in the freezer once the packet has been opened.

MEXICAN OREGANO:

Distinctively different in flavour from the dull-smelling pots of the standard dried herb you find on the supermarket shelf, Mexican oregano has a pungent citrus smell and flavour. Use along with dried chilli. You can find this online at Sous Chef.

PICKLED JALAPEÑOS:

Sold in jars, these consist of fresh green jalapeños that have usually been pickled in a combo of white wine vinegar, sugar, salt and various aromatics. Make your own for a more complex flavour (page 106).

TORTILLAS

When buying tortillas made from either corn (maize) or wheat there are several to choose from. The recipes in this book specify standard soft corn tortillas, but they would work with the other varieties of tortillas too. Just make sure you stick to the size specified in each recipe.

BLUE CORN TORTILLAS:

Less easy to source than the other varieties, these tortillas are greyish-blue in colour and have a richer, nuttier flavour. Lovely with fish and hot chilli.

FLOUR TORTILLAS:

Larger than the other tortillas and available in all supermarkets, these are only really used for quesadillas or burritos.

SOFT CORN TORTILLAS:

Sweetish in flavour and easy to pick up from your local corner shop or supermarket, soft corn tortillas are generally made with yellow corn flour. You can buy them in 20cm (8in) and 15cm (6in) sizes. They also work well deep-fried or baked for making into tortilla chips (pages 42–43).

WHITE CORN TORTILLAS:

The most traditional type of tortilla. You can buy these online and they usually come in the classic 15cm (6in) size. Lighter in colour and milder in flavour, these are perfect with most taco recipes.

TORTILLA CHIPS

BLUE CORN TORTILLA CHIPS:

Dark blue and thicker in texture than standard corn (maize) tortilla chips, as well as sweeter and subtler in flavour, these are perfect for dipping into a pot of homemade guacamole or Pico de Gallo Salsa (pages 102 and 95).

CANTINA CHIPS:

These are made in the traditional way from pressed white corn tortillas, creating a more delicate tortilla chip. Seriously worth looking around the supermarket for these guys. They are available in various brands, including Manomasa.

CORN TORTILLA CHIPS:

The most common type of tortilla chip, these are a creamy yellow in colour and often come sprinkled with salt.

FRESH PRODUCE

BUTTERMILK:

Essentially a cultured milk, this is thin and yoghurt-like in consistency with a slightly sour, buttery taste. Use for marinating fried chicken (page 34) or for creamy dressings.

FRESH CHILLIES (GREEN AND RED):

Whatever colour they are, chillies can vary dramatically in heat. Slice a piece off the end of a chilli before using and lightly dab on your bottom lip to test its heat. Always make sure you follow the instructions in a recipe as to whether to keep them seeded or deseeded, as this will affect the level of heat.

JALAPEÑO CHILLIES:

Widely available, the jalapeño is a mild Latin American chilli pepper. With a fruity flavour, it's great pickled (page 106) or sliced and scattered over tacos.

MEXICAN CREMA:

Crema is a dairy product that is only available in Mexico. For the recipes here, instructions are given for making your own version by combining soured cream and good-quality mayonnaise. It's delicious with chipotle paste swirled through it and served with tacos.

QUESO FRESCO:

A mild creamy cheese not dissimilar from a mild soft goat's cheese. Try it crumbled on charred corn on the cob (page 74). Available online.

SOURED CREAM:

A key ingredient in many nacho dishes and a refreshing coolant for hot chilli-based dishes. Try to use the full-fat variety – it's much creamier and tastier!

WHITE ONIONS:

Milder than the common yellow onion, with a pale flesh and white papery exterior, these are easier to eat raw and work well as a garnish or thinly sliced and tossed into a salad.

HOW TO SERVE THE RECIPES

NACHOS

The serving quantities for these recipes depend entirely on how you fancy eating them! Where 'Serves 4–6' is specified, this indicates that the recipe will serve four hungry people as a starter or six as a sharing snack, unless otherwise stated. Where 'Serves 2–4' is given, this means the recipe will serve two as a starter or four as a snack to share. Recipes serving four indicate smaller portions, hence would work well as a starter. If you want to serve any of these recipes as a main dish, they would be best combined with a taco and a snack recipe as part of a sharing table.

TACOS

The choice is yours on how to serve these tacos. The taco itself is simply a vehicle for layering exciting flavours. What's lovely is to pile the toppings into bowls, keep the tortillas warm on a plate and let your guests build their own tacos. That way, those who prefer them spicier, meatier or more vegetal are free to choose to their own taste! Alternatively, you can assemble the tacos and take them to the table. Make sure you have a good supply of paper napkins at hand; tacos have a fatal tendency to eject some of their delicious fillings straight onto your brand new white blouse!

Most of the tacos in this book serve 4–6 people, six as a starter (i.e. two tacos each) or four as a main (three tacos each). If you serve the tacos as a main, you might want to add a nacho recipe or a Mexicana snack or two. The recipes that just serve four are intended solely as a main dish.

A GOOD COMBINATION OF DISHES FOR SIX PEOPLE MIGHT BE:

- ULTIMATE CLASSIC NACHOS
  (PAGE 44)

- PORK CARNITAS WITH PINEAPPLE SALSA
  (PAGE 36)

- FIERY HABANERO CHICKEN WINGS
  (PAGE 82)

- CHARRED FRUIT WITH POMEGRANATE AND
  VANILLA MASCARPONE OR CHURROS (PAGES 121
  AND 110)

- CLASSIC MARGARITA
  (PAGE 124)

The idea of this book is to combine dishes to your liking, and create a fun sharing table of Mexicana flavours. So get mixing and matching!

1

TACOS

HOMEMADE SOFT CORN TORTILLAS

Making a corn tortilla can be a little tricky to master at first, but once you get into the swing of things you'll be churning them out in no time. Masa harina, a fine flour made from corn (maize), is essential to this recipe. It's available online and in specialist food shops. A good tip is to keep the flour in the freezer once opened, as it goes bad pretty quickly. It's also easier to get a better-shaped tortilla if you use a tortilla press, which you can easily order online.

MAKES 12 X 15CM (6IN) TORTILLAS
PREP: 15 MINUTES, PLUS RESTING
COOK: 15 MINUTES

220g (7½oz/1¾ cups) masa harina flour

½ tsp fine salt

260–270ml (9–9½fl oz/generous 1 cup) warm water

You may need a tortilla press (optional)

1. In a large bowl, combine the flour and salt. Make a well in the centre and pour in 260ml (9fl oz/1 cup) of the warm water. Combine with a wooden spoon; you should be left with a soft dough that is easy to handle and not too sticky – add more water if it feels dry. Knead briefly until the dough is smooth and easy to handle. Place in a bowl, cover with a clean tea towel and leave to rest for 30 minutes in a warm spot.

2. Divide the dough into 12 even-sized pieces and roll each piece into a ball. Cut a plastic sandwich bag in half to create two square sheets. Place a dough ball between the plastic sheets and press in a tortilla press, or roll with a rolling pin, into a round about 15cm (6in) in diameter. If you're using a tortilla press, you may need to turn the tortilla and re-press several times to obtain the desired size. Repeat with the remaining dough balls. Set the tortillas aside in a stack, separating each one with a piece of baking parchment to stop them sticking to each other.

3. Heat a heavy-based frying pan (skillet) over a medium heat. Cook the tortillas one at a time for around 30 seconds on each side or until beginning to brown slightly. Stack the tortillas up and cover with foil; this will help them to keep warm and soft until ready to use. If not eating the tortillas immediately, keep them wrapped in foil and store in an airtight container for up to 24 hours, then reheat on both sides in a small dry frying pan.

THRIFTY TACOS WITH CANNED PINEAPPLE SALSA

When there's not much in the house except some dusty cans in the back of the cupboard and a few leftover bits and pieces in the fridge, it's easy to lose inspiration, but a soft taco topped with something tasty from a tin is a seriously yummy option. Top with any tail-ends of cheese from the fridge and a dollop of natural yoghurt, and feel free to swap any of the salad ingredients with whatever you have to hand.

SERVES 4
PREP: 20 MINUTES
COOK: 20 MINUTES

2 tbsp olive oil

1 large red onion, finely sliced

1 red or yellow (bell) pepper, deseeded and sliced

2 tsp sweet smoked paprika

1 tsp hot paprika or medium chilli powder

1 tsp ground coriander

2 fat garlic cloves, finely grated

3 x 400g cans mixed beans, drained and rinsed

2 large tomatoes, deseeded and chopped

8 x 20cm (8in) soft corn tortillas

3 Baby Gem lettuces, shredded

1 bunch of spring onions (scallions), sliced

150g (5oz) cherry tomatoes, halved

150g (5oz) Gouda or Cheddar, grated

120g (4½oz/½ cup) natural yoghurt

Salt and black pepper

Chilli sauce, to serve

CANNED PINEAPPLE SALSA

6 canned pineapple rings, drained and cut into chunks

1 heaped tsp chilli flakes

½ small red onion, very finely chopped

1 small handful of coriander (cilantro), finely chopped

1. Heat the olive oil in a non-stick frying pan (skillet) over a medium heat. Add the onion and pepper with a pinch of salt and fry for 10–12 minutes or until beginning to soften. Stir through the paprika (sweet and hot) and coriander, along with the garlic, and cook for 1 minute. Stir through the beans and tomatoes and cook for another 5 minutes. Season to taste with salt and pepper.

2. In a small bowl, combine the pineapple chunks with the chilli flakes, onion and coriander. Toss together the lettuce, spring onions and cherry tomatoes in a serving bowl.

3. Warm the tortillas through in a small dry frying pan over a medium-high heat, keeping a stack warm, wrapped in foil, in a low oven while you heat the rest. Take these to the table, along with the warm beans, pineapple salsa, salad bowl, grated cheese, yoghurt and chilli sauce, and let everyone assemble their own tacos with anything they fancy!

BREAKFAST TACOS

These easy breakfast tacos are just the ticket on a lazy Saturday morning or even for lunch or dinner! If you're veggie, swap the crispy bacon for thick slices of milky halloumi cheese, either grilled (broiled) or charred in a griddle pan.

SERVES 4
PREP: 10 MINUTES
COOK: 25 MINUTES

400g (14oz) small vine-ripened
  tomatoes

½ tbsp olive oil

12 rashers (slices) of smoked streaky
  bacon or 1 x 250g (9oz) block of
  halloumi, sliced

300g (11oz) baby spinach

3 tbsp double (heavy) cream

A pinch of freshly grated nutmeg

1 tbsp sunflower or vegetable oil

4 large free-range eggs

4 x 20cm (8in) soft corn tortillas

4 tbsp chilli jam or Smoky Chipotle
  and Tomato Chutney (page 100)

Salt and black pepper

1. Keeping the tomatoes attached to the vine, rub them with the olive oil and season generously with salt and pepper. Heat a non-stick frying pan (skillet) over a medium-high heat. Add the tomatoes and fry for 5–6 minutes until blistered. Set aside.

2. Preheat the grill (broiler) to high. Line a baking tray (cookie sheet) with foil and lay the bacon on it. Grill for 4–6 minutes, turning halfway, or until the bacon is golden brown and crisp. If using halloumi, grill on each side for 1 minute or until evenly golden brown.

3. Meanwhile, place the spinach in a pan over a medium heat and add 1 tablespoon of water, cover with a lid and cook for 4–5 minutes until wilted. Transfer to a colander and squeeze out any excess liquid by pressing the spinach with the back of a wooden spoon. Return to a clean pan, along with the cream, nutmeg and some salt and pepper, and warm through over a low heat.

4. Heat the sunflower oil until hot in a non-stick frying pan over a medium heat. Once starting to bubble, crack in the eggs and fry until crisp around the edges with a just-set runny yolk.

5. Warm the tortillas through in a small dry frying pan over a medium-high heat, keeping a stack warm, wrapped in foil, in a low oven while you heat the rest. Top each one with a fried egg, three crisp bacon rashers or slices of halloumi, a couple of charred tomatoes, a spoonful of spinach and a generous dollop of chilli jam or chipotle chutney. These might be a little fiddly to eat with your hands, as you would other tacos, so grab a knife and fork and a couple of napkins before digging in!

HUEVOS RANCHEROS

Huevos rancheros are a traditional Mexican breakfast, consisting of warmed tortillas with a spicy topping, such as black beans, and fried eggs. Add to this sweet peppers cooked with a warming hint of coriander and the cooling creamy avocado for a cracking weekend brekkie!

SERVES 4
PREP: 15 MINUTES
COOK: 20 MINUTES

2 tbsp olive oil

1 yellow (bell) pepper, deseeded and thinly sliced

1 orange (bell) pepper, deseeded and thinly sliced

1 garlic clove, crushed

1 tsp ground coriander

1 x 400g can black or pinto beans, drained and rinsed

180g (6oz) cherry tomatoes, quartered

2 medium-sized fresh red chillies, one finely chopped the other sliced

Juice of 1 lime

2 tbsp vegetable oil

4 medium free-range eggs

4 x 20cm (8in) soft corn tortillas

Flesh of 2 medium avocados, sliced

Salt and black pepper

Cholula or other chilli sauce, to serve (optional)

1. Heat the olive oil in a non-stick pan over a medium heat. Add the peppers and fry gently for 5 minutes. Add the garlic and ground coriander and continue cooking for another minute. Stir through the beans, tomatoes and chopped chilli and cook everything for a further 5 minutes or until just beginning to break down. Season to taste with salt and pepper and add the lime juice.

2. Heat the vegetable oil in a non-stick frying pan (skillet) over a medium heat. When the oil is hot crack in the eggs and cook until crispy around the edges and the yolks are just set but still runny.

3. Warm the tortillas through in a small dry frying pan over a medium-high heat, keeping a stack warm, wrapped in foil, in a low oven while you heat the rest. Divide the bean mixture among them, top each with a fried egg and some sliced avocado. Finish with a good shake of hot sauce if you like it spicy!

CHARRED SPRING ONION AND MARINATED FETA TACOS

Feta can be transformed just by leaving it for an hour or two in a delicious marinade of flavoured olive oil. Paired with griddled spring onions, these tacos make for a veggie delight!

SERVES 4–6
PREP: 15 MINUTES, PLUS MARINATING
COOK: 20 MINUTES

1 x 200g (7oz) block of feta

100ml (3½fl oz/½ cup) extra-virgin olive oil

½ tsp chilli flakes

Leaves of 1 small bunch of dill, torn

1 lemon

2 tbsp olive oil

24 spring onions (scallions), trimmed

400g (14oz) chard or spinach

2 tbsp crème fraîche

Leaves of 1 small bunch of flat-leaf parsley, roughly chopped

12 x 15cm (6cm) soft corn tortillas, homemade (page 16) or shop-bought

1 fresh red chilli, finely sliced

Salt and black pepper

1. Place the feta in a shallow bowl. Whisk together the olive oil and chilli flakes with half the dill and the pared zest of half the lemon. Pour the mixture over the feta and leave to marinate in the fridge for 1–2 hours.

2. Wash any dirt or grit off the spring onions and pat dry. Heat a ridged griddle pan or heavy-based frying pan (skillet) over a high heat until almost at smoking point. Drizzle a little olive oil over the spring onions, then add to the pan and cook in batches for 3–4 minutes on each side until blistered and beginning to soften. Remove and keep warm.

3. Roughly slice the chard or spinach, place in a steamer or in a saucepan with 1 tablespoon of water, covered with a lid and steam for 5 minutes or until wilted. Remove from the steamer/pan and squeeze out any excess water by placing in a colander and pressing down with the back of a wooden spoon. Combine with the finely grated zest of the remaining lemon half, the crème fraîche and parsley. Season to taste with salt and pepper.

4. Warm the tortillas through in a small dry frying pan over a medium-high heat, keeping a stack warm, wrapped in foil, in a low oven while you heat the rest. Top each one with a spoonful of the wilted greens, a couple of spring onions and some of the marinated feta crumbled into pieces. Drizzle over a little of the marinade and finish with some of the remaining dill and the sliced red chilli scattered over.

ANCHO SMOKED TOFU AND MANGO TACOS

Thick wedges of smoked tofu are a great substitute for meat. For these tacos the tofu wedges are marinated in a mild ancho chilli paste, fried and then piled into tortillas with a fresh mango and chilli salsa. Smoked tofu is available online and in many of the mainstream supermarkets.

SERVES 4–6
PREP: 25 MINUTES, PLUS MARINATING
COOK: 10 MINUTES

2 x 200g (7oz) blocks of smoked tofu, cut into slices 1cm (½in) thick

1 tbsp ancho or standard medium chilli powder

2 tsp sweet smoked paprika

1 tsp ground cumin

2 tbsp olive oil

12 x 15cm (6in) soft corn tortillas, homemade (page 16) or shop-bought

½ small red cabbage, shredded

2 fresh green jalapeño peppers, sliced

Guacamole (page 102), to serve

Cholula or other chilli sauce, to serve (optional)

FOR THE MANGO SALSA

Flesh of 2 large ripe mangoes

1 small fresh red chilli, deseeded and finely chopped

Leaves of ½ small bunch of coriander (cilantro), shredded

Zest and juice of 1 large lime

1. In a large bowl, toss together the tofu, chilli powder, paprika and cumin. Cover and set aside for 30 minutes.

2. Next prepare the mango salsa. Chop the mangoes into 2cm (¾in) cubes, place in a bowl and toss the with the red chilli, coriander and lime zest and juice, then set aside.

3. Heat the olive oil in a large non-stick frying pan (skillet) or griddle pan over a high heat. Add the tofu and fry for 5 minutes, turning halfway through, until crisp and brown on each side.

4. Warm the tortillas through in a small dry frying pan over a medium-high heat, keeping a stack warm, wrapped in foil, in a low oven while you heat the rest. Top each one with some of the spiced tofu, a little of the mango salsa, some shredded red cabbage, sliced jalapeño and a spoonful of guacamole. Serve with a shake of extra-hot sauce, if you like it spicier!

SPICED SQUASH, FETA AND MINT CHERMOULA TACOS

These tacos combine sweet autumnal nuggets of butternut squash with a punchy green chermoula sauce. If you're vegan, simply remove the feta from the recipe; these are equally delicious with or without it.

SERVES 4–6
PREP: 20 MINUTES
COOK: 30–35 MINUTES

1 large butternut squash

2 tsp chipotle or standard chilli flakes

2 tsp sweet smoked paprika

1 tsp ground coriander

6 tbsp olive oil

2 small bunches of mint

½ small bunch of coriander (cilantro)

Zest and juice of 1 lemon

¼ tsp caster (superfine) sugar

1 small garlic clove, chopped

½ tsp cumin seeds

12 x 15cm (6in) soft corn tortillas, homemade (page 16) or shop-bought

100g (3½oz) feta, crumbled

1 handful of mixed seeds

Salt and black pepper

1. Preheat the oven to 200°C (180°fan)/400°F/gas 6.

2. Halve, peel and deseed the squash, then cut the flesh into 2cm (¾in) chunks. In a large bowl, mix together the chilli flakes, paprika, ground coriander and 1 tablespoon of the olive oil. Add the squash pieces and toss in the spice mixture, seasoning generously with salt and pepper, then arrange on a baking tray (cookie sheet) in a single layer.

3. Place in the oven and roast for 25–30 minutes, tossing halfway through. The squash is cooked when a table knife can be easily inserted into one chunk without resistance.

4. Place the remaining olive oil in a food processor or blender with the mint, coriander, lemon zest and juice, sugar, garlic and cumin seeds and whizz until smooth. Season to taste with salt.

5. Warm the tortillas through in a small dry frying pan (skillet) over a medium-high heat, keeping a stack warm, wrapped in foil, in a low oven while you heat the rest. Top each one with some of the spiced roasted squash, mint chermoula, crumbled feta and a sprinkling of the crunchy seeds.

BLACK BEAN, CHARRED CORN AND AVOCADO CREMA TACOS

You don't necessarily need a pot of soured cream to make a silky, Mexican-style crema; just whizz an avocado with lime juice until super smooth. These guys are veggie packed and totally vegan.

SERVES 4–6
PREP: 35 MINUTES
COOK: 20 MINUTES

3 tbsp olive oil

1 bunch of spring onions (scallions), finely sliced

1 mild fresh green chilli, deseeded and finely chopped

2 fat garlic cloves, crushed

1 tbsp coriander seeds, crushed

½ tsp hot smoked paprika

2 corn on the cob

2 x 400g cans black beans, drained and rinsed

Leaves of ½ large bunch of coriander (cilantro), shredded, plus extra to serve

12 x 15cm (6in) soft corn tortillas, homemade (page 16) or shop-bought

5 radishes, thinly sliced

2 fresh red chillies, finely sliced

Salt and black pepper

FOR THE AVOCADO CREMA

Flesh of 2 medium-sized ripe avocados, roughly chopped

Zest and juice of 2 limes

250ml (9fl oz/1 cup) water

1 heaped tsp fine salt

1. Heat 1 tablespoon of the oil in a large non-stick frying pan (skillet) over a medium heat. Add half the spring onions and the green chilli and fry for 3 minutes. Tip in the garlic, coriander and paprika and fry for a further minute. Remove from the heat and set aside.

2. Next add all the ingredients for the avocado crema to a blender or the small bowl of a food processor and blitz until very smooth. Transfer to a serving bowl and set aside.

3. Bring a large saucepan of water to the boil. Add the corn on the cob and boil for 3 minutes. Drain in a colander set over the pan and leave to steam dry for 5 minutes. Heat a ridged griddle or non-stick frying pan over a high heat until almost at smoking point. Add the corn to the pan and cook for 7–10 minutes, turning regularly until blackened and charred. Once cooked, slice off kernels in chunks from the side of each corn on the cob using a sharp knife and set aside in a bowl.

4. Pat the rinsed black beans thoroughly dry with kitchen paper (paper towels) and stir into to the spring onion mixture. Warm through over a medium heat for 5 minutes. Season to taste with salt and pepper and fold through the chopped coriander.

5. Warm the tortillas through in a small dry frying pan over a medium-high heat, keeping a stack warm, wrapped in foil, in a low oven while you heat the rest. Top each one with a spoonful of the spiced beans and charred corn kernels, a drizzle of avocado crema and a sprinkling of coriander, sliced radish and red chilli. Pop any remaining crema in a bowl and serve on the side.

CRAB AND AVOCADO TACOS

These little mouthfuls of creamy crab, zesty lime and punchy chilli are an absolute doddle to make. Use fresh crab if you can – it'll taste delicious. But if you can't get hold of it, a can of good-quality crabmeat will work well too.

SERVES 4–6
PREP: 15 MINUTES
COOK: 5 MINUTES

450g (1lb) white crabmeat

2 medium-sized fresh red chillies, deseeded and finely chopped

2 tbsp good-quality mayonnaise

2 tbsp crème fraîche

½ tsp Dijon mustard

½ tsp Tabasco sauce, plus extra to serve

Zest and juice of 1 large lime, plus extra wedges to serve

12 x 15cm (6in) soft corn tortillas, homemade (page 16) or shop-bought

Flesh of 2 medium-sized ripe avocados, sliced

1 handful of salad cress, snipped

Salt and black pepper

1. Place the crabmeat and half the chopped chillies in a bowl and add the mayonnaise, crème fraîche, mustard, Tabasco sauce and lime zest and juice. Gently fold everything together and season to taste with salt and pepper.

2. Warm the tortillas through in a small dry frying pan (skillet) over a medium-high heat, keeping a stack warm, wrapped in foil, in a low oven while you heat the rest. Top each one with a spoonful of the crab mixture, a few slices of avocado, the salad cress and remaining chillies. Serve with wedges of lime. If you like it spicier, slosh a little extra Tabasco over the top before eating.

BAJA FISH TACOS

Originating in sunny California, Baja fish tacos consist of white fish deep-fried in a crisp batter and piled onto tortillas with crunchy red cabbage and lime. If you're going to make one tacos recipe for your mates, this is the one!

SERVES 4–6
PREP: 20 MINUTES, PLUS CHILLING
COOK: 20 MINUTES

150g (5oz/1¼ cups) plain
   (all-purpose) flour

75g (3oz/¾ cup) cornflour (cornstarch)

1 tsp sweet smoked paprika

200ml–250ml (7–9fl oz/¾–1 cup) ice-
   cold beer (such as Mexican Sol)

600g (1lb 5oz) skinless and boneless
   cod loin, cut into 3cm (1¼in) chunks

1.5 litres (2½ pints/6 cups) vegetable oil

½ large red cabbage, finely shredded

Juice of 1 lime, plus wedges to serve

Leaves of 1 small bunch of coriander
   (cilantro), roughly chopped

12 x 15cm (6in) soft corn tortillas,
   homemade (page 16) or shop-bought

6 tbsp Chipotle Aioli or Zesty Lime
   Aioli (page 107)

1 large fresh red chilli, finely sliced

6 tbsp Pink Pickled Onions (page 104)

Fine salt

1. Sift the flour, cornflour and paprika into a bowl and add ½ teaspoon of salt. Make a well in the centre and slowly whisk in enough of the cold beer to create a thick batter. Cover and set aside in the fridge for 30 minutes to rest.

2. In a serving bowl, toss together the shredded cabbage with the lime juice and half the coriander. Season generously with salt.

3. Heat the vegetable oil in a deep-fryer, or in a large, deep heavy-based saucepan filled no more than two-thirds full, until the oil reaches 190°C (375°F) on a cooking thermometer. Alternatively, drop in a small cube of bread to check that the oil is hot enough; it should turn golden brown within 10 seconds.

4. Dip each piece of cod into the batter and gently shake off any excess. Carefully place in the hot oil using a slotted spoon and cook in batches, for 4 minutes per batch. Remove with the slotted spoon and drain on kitchen paper (paper towels) while you cook the remaining fish.

5. Warm the tortillas through in a small dry frying pan (skillet) over a medium-high heat, keeping a stack warm, wrapped in foil, in a low oven while you heat the rest. Top each one with a smear of aioli, followed by some of the battered fish, dressed red cabbage and sliced red chilli. Finish with a bundle of pickled onions and some of the remaining coriander, plus a wedge of lime to squeeze over.

CRISPY SQUID AND SUNSHINE SALAD TACOS

Perfect for a summer lunch, corn tortillas are spread with a generous slick of homemade Chipotle Aioli (page 107) before being topped with squid that's been tossed in seasoned flour and deep-fried until crisp. The tacos are then piled with handfuls of fresh herby salad mixed with juicy orange segments and pomegranate seeds.

SERVES 4–6
PREP: 35 MINUTES
COOK: 15 MINUTES

500g (1lb 2oz) squid, gutted and cleaned

1.5 litres (2½ pints/6 cups) sunflower oil

5 heaped tbsp plain (all-purpose) flour

½ tsp hot chilli powder

2 tsp sweet smoked paprika

12 x 15cm (6cm) soft corn tortillas, homemade (page 16) or shop-bought

6 tbsp Chipotle Aioli (page 107) or 5 tbsp good-quality mayonnaise mixed with 1 tbsp chipotle chilli paste

FOR THE SALAD

Leaves of 1 large bunch of parsley, torn

Leaves of 1 small bunch of coriander (cilantro), torn

1 large banana shallot, sliced into thin rounds

2 small oranges

2 large handfuls of pomegranate seeds

Juice of 2 limes

2 tbsp extra-virgin olive oil

Fine salt and black pepper

1. Cut the squid into 1cm (½in) rounds, keeping any tentacles in nice whole pieces. Set aside for later.

2. Prepare the salad by tossing together the torn herb leaves and the sliced shallot. Use a serrated knife to cut the skin and pith from the oranges, then break into segments and toss with the herbs and pomegranate seeds. In a small jug or bowl, whisk together the lime juice and olive oil, along with a good pinch of salt and pepper, and set aside to toss through the salad later.

3. Heat the sunflower oil in a deep-fryer, or in a large, deep heavy-based saucepan filled no more than two-thirds full, until the oil reaches 190–200°C (375–400°F) on a cooking thermometer. Alternatively, drop in a small cube of bread to check that the oil is hot enough; it should turn golden brown within 10 seconds.

4. Pat the prepared squid dry with kitchen paper (paper towels) to remove any excess moisture. In a bowl, mix together the flour, chilli powder and paprika with 2 teaspoons of salt and ¼ teaspoon of freshly ground black pepper. In small batches, toss the squid in the flour mixture and deep-fry for 1–2 minutes per batch or until light golden brown and crispy. Remove with a slotted spoon and drain on kitchen paper. Sprinkle with a little more salt to keep them crisp.

5. Warm the tortillas through in a small dry frying pan (skillet) over a medium-high heat, keeping a stack warm, wrapped in foil, in a low oven while you heat the rest. Toss the salad in the lime dressing, then spread the chipotle aioli over the warmed tortillas, top with the crispy squid and a good handful of the fruity citrus salad.

FISH FINGER TACOS WITH QUICK PICKLED CUCUMBER

Comforting fish finger sarnies have been given the taco treatment in this recipe. Japanese panko breadcrumbs are best to use as they give a lovely crunchy coating, but if you can't get hold of any, you can make your own by whizzing up some stale bread and drying out the crumbs on a baking tray for 10 minutes in a moderate oven. For super-crispy fish fingers, deep-fry them in hot oil for 3–4 minutes until golden brown.

SERVES 4–6
PREP: 35 MINUTES, PLUS CHILLING
COOK: 15 MINUTES

6 x 250g (9oz) thick haddock fillets

5 tbsp plain (all-purpose) flour

2 large free-range eggs, beaten

150g (5oz/3 cups) panko breadcrumbs

2 tbsp vegetable oil

30g (1oz/2 tbsp) unsalted butter

12 x 15cm (6in) soft corn tortillas, homemade (page 16) or shop-bought

2 Baby Gem lettuces, leaves separated

½ small red onion, finely chopped

Salt and black pepper

Good-quality mayonnaise, to serve

Cholula or other chilli sauce, or ketchup, to serve

FOR THE PICKLED CUCUMBER

80ml (3fl oz/⅓ cup) white wine vinegar

40ml (1½fl oz/⅛ cup) water

½ tsp salt

1 tbsp caster (superfine) sugar

1 tsp black peppercorns

½ cucumber, sliced into thin rounds

Leaves of ½ small bunch of dill, chopped, plus extra to serve

1. First make the pickled cucumber. Place the vinegar and water in a small pan with the salt, sugar and peppercorns. Bring to a simmer and swirl the pan until the sugar has dissolved, then remove from the heat and allow to cool down for 10 minutes. Toss the cucumber and dill together in a bowl. Pour over the cooled pickling liquid and set aside, covered, in the fridge for 30 minutes.

2. Cut each fish fillet into two chunky fingers. Place the flour, beaten eggs and breadcrumbs in three separate bowls. Season the flour generously with salt and pepper. Line a baking tray (cookie sheet) with baking parchment, then dip each piece of fish in the flour, followed by the egg and then in the breadcrumbs to coat. Place on the lined tray and chill in the fridge until needed.

3. Heat the vegetable oil and butter in a non-stick frying pan (skillet) over a medium heat until the butter melts and begins to foam. Add the fish fingers and fry on each side for 3–4 minutes or until golden brown and crisp. Remove from the heat, sprinkle with a little salt and set aside on kitchen paper (paper towels).

4. Warm the tortillas through in a small dry frying pan over a medium-high heat, keeping a stack warm, wrapped in foil, in a low oven while you heat the rest. Top each one with a slick of mayonnaise, a fish finger, some pickled cucumber, a couple of lettuce leaves, some red onion and any extra dill fronds. Splatter over some chilli sauce or relive those childhood memories with a squirt of ketchup!

BLISTERED CHORIZO AND POTATO TACOS

Spicy chorizo and fried potatoes are a match made in heaven. Frying potatoes in butter and oil makes them golden and crispy on the outside and soft in the middle. Don't be tempted to turn the heat up too high on these, though; they work better when left to cook for longer over a medium heat.

SERVES 4–6
PREP: 30 MINUTES
COOK: 35 MINUTES

750g (1lb 10oz) waxy potatoes (such as Désirée), peeled and cut into 2cm (¾in) cubes

170g (6oz) spicy chorizo, cubed

25g (1oz/2 tbsp) unsalted butter

2 tbsp olive oil, plus extra if needed

4 fat garlic cloves, peeled

1 sprig rosemary

½ tsp hot smoked paprika

130g (4½oz/generous ½ cup) soured cream

2 tbsp good-quality mayonnaise

½ tbsp chipotle chilli paste

12 x 15cm (6in) soft corn tortillas, homemade (page 16) or shop-bought

Leaves of 1 small bunch of coriander (cilantro), shredded

Salt and black pepper

Pico de Gallo Salsa (page 95), to serve

1. Bring a large pan of salted water to the boil, add the potatoes and parboil for 3 minutes, then drain in a colander and allow to steam dry for 5 minutes.

2. Heat a large non-stick frying pan (skillet) over a medium heat. Add the chorizo and fry for 5 minutes or until golden and crisp. Remove from the pan with a slotted spoon and set aside for later.

3. In the same pan, heat the butter and oil together over a low–medium heat until the butter melts and begins to foam. Add the parboiled potatoes to the pan and nestle in the garlic and rosemary. Sprinkle over the paprika and season generously with salt and pepper. Cook for 25–30 minutes over a medium heat, turning every so often, until the potatoes are golden brown. If the pan starts to look a little dry, drizzle in a glug more oil. Add the chorizo back to the pan to warm through.

4. In a small bowl, combine the soured cream, mayonnaise and chipotle chilli paste and set aside.

5. Warm the tortillas through in a small dry frying pan over a medium-high heat, keeping a stack warm, wrapped in foil, in a low oven while you heat the rest. Mix the shredded coriander together with the potato mixture and pile some on top of each tortilla, followed by a spoonful of pico de gallo salsa and a drizzle of the chipotle cream. Fold up and enjoy!

BUTTERMILK FRIED CHICKEN AND PICKLED JALAPEÑO AIOLI TACOS

A crunchy golden, spiced-coated piece of tender chicken is quite the thing at the best of times, but is even more spectacular rolled in a warm tortilla with a smear of homemade pickled jalapeño aioli and topped with sliced chillies. Go to a little more effort and make these for your mates on a Friday night, but make sure you have a cooking thermometer. It's essential for checking that the oil is at the right temperature so that the chicken is beautifully crisp on the outside and cooked all the way through to the middle.

SERVES 4-6
PREP: 35 MINUTES, PLUS MARINATING
COOK: 40 MINUTES

8 skinless and boneless chicken thighs
400ml (14fl oz/1⅔ cup) buttermilk
3 tsp fine salt
100g (3½oz/¾ cup) plain
    (all-purpose) flour
50g (2oz/½ cup) wholemeal (whole
    wheat) flour
50g (2oz/½ cup) cornflour (cornstarch)
½ tsp baking powder
½ tsp hot smoked paprika
1 tsp sweet smoked paprika
1 tsp garlic powder
A good pinch of ground cloves
2 litres (3½ pints/8 cups) vegetable oil
12 x 15cm (6in) soft corn tortillas,
    homemade (page 16) or shop-bought
6 tbsp Pickled Jalapeño Aioli (page 107)
1 large bunch of coriander (cilantro)
1 large fresh red chilli, finely sliced
1 fresh jalapeño chilli, finely sliced
1 small white onion, finely chopped

1. Begin by cutting each chicken thigh into three chunky strips, then place in a bowl and add the buttermilk and 1 teaspoon of the salt. Cover the bowl and set aside in the fridge for 24 hours to marinate.

2. The next day toss the two flours with the cornflour, baking powder, paprika (hot and sweet), garlic powder, ground cloves and the remaining salt. Have a tray lined and ready with greaseproof paper and a second one lined with kitchen paper (paper towels).

3. Remove the chicken strips one at a time from the buttermilk, shake off any excess liquid and drop into the dry mix, tossing until well coated. Transfer to the tray lined with greaseproof paper while you continue coating the remaining chicken.

4. Heat the oil in a deep-fryer, or in a large, deep heavy-based saucepan filled no more than two-thirds full, until the oil reaches 180°C (350°F) on a cooking thermometer. Add the chicken 4–5 pieces at a time and deep-fry for 6–7 minutes per batch until deep golden brown and cooked all the way through. Remove with a slotted spoon and set aside in a warm place on the lined tray while you cook the remaining chicken pieces.

5. Warm the tortillas through in a small dry frying pan (skillet) over a medium-high heat, keeping a stack wrapped in foil, in a low oven while you heat the rest. Smear each one with a spoonful of the aioli, then top with some of the fried chicken, torn coriander and sliced chillies and onion. Wrap up and enjoy!

PORK CARNITAS WITH PINEAPPLE SALSA

Pork shoulder is slow-cooked in this recipe until meltingly soft before being piled onto tortillas and topped with a fresh, sharp pineapple salsa. This is definitely one to try for pure Mexicana authenticity. Serve up these tacos to friends, along with some ice-cold margaritas (pages 124–127), to get the fiesta going!

SERVES 4–6
PREP: 40 MINUTES, PLUS CHILLING
COOK: 3½–4 HOURS

250g (9oz/1¼ cups) lard

1.2kg (2lb 10oz) boned pork shoulder, cut into 5cm (2in) chunks

1 large white onion, sliced

½ tbsp coriander seeds, crushed

½ tbsp ground cumin

1 tbsp fennel seeds

2 bay leaves

Juice of 1 large orange

300ml (10fl oz/1¼ cups) chicken stock

12 x 15cm (6in) soft corn tortillas, homemade (page 16) or shop-bought

Salt

Pink Pickled Onions (page 104), to serve

Guacamole (page 102), to serve

FOR THE PINEAPPLE SALSA

250g (9oz) fresh pineapple flesh, cut into 1cm (½in) cubes

½ small red onion, very finely chopped

½ large fresh red chilli, deseeded and finely chopped

Leaves of 1 small handful of coriander (cilantro), chopped, plus extra to serve

Leaves of 1 small handful of mint, chopped

Zest and juice of 1 large lime

1. Place a large heavy-based saucepan (with a lid) over a high heat. Melt a spoonful of the lard in the pan and fry the pork in several batches, using more of the lard each time, for around 5 minutes per batch until evenly browned.

2. Place all the browned meat back in the pan, along with the onion, spices, bay leaves, orange juice, chicken stock and 2 teaspoons of salt. Cover the pan with the lid, leaving it slightly ajar, and bring to the boil. Once boiling, lower to a simmer and cook very gently for 3–3½ hours or until the meat is falling apart.

3. Combine the pineapple in a bowl with the red onion, chilli, coriander and mint. Stir through the lime zest and juice and ½ teaspoon of salt and set aside, covered, in the fridge for 30 minutes.

4. Drain the pork in a colander set over a bowl, discard any really large pieces of the fat, then transfer the meat to a chopping board and pull apart with two forks. Heat a non-stick frying pan (skillet) over a high heat and add the meat to the pan. Fry for 5–6 minutes, turning the pork regularly, until parts begin to turn golden and crispy.

5. Warm the tortillas through in a small dry frying pan over a medium-high heat, keeping a stack warm, wrapped in foil, in a low oven while you heat the rest. Take the pan of pork to the table and top each tortilla with the pulled meat and a spoonful of the cooking juices, along with some of the pineapple salsa, pickled onions, guacamole and a sprinkling of coriander.

CARNE ASADA TACOS

Carne asada, a Latin American dish, simply means 'grilled (broiled) meat' in Spanish. In this recipe the type of beef used is bavette – a delicious, highly flavoured, loose-textured cut that is easily obtainable from your local butcher. If you can't get hold of it, however, simply swap it for two or three large sirloin steaks. The meat is marinated and charred in a griddle pan, then piled onto warm tortillas and topped with zesty garnishes. These are drizzled with a punchy green sauce and a fresh tomato salsa. If you fancy it a little hotter, add a chopped red chilli to the green sauce before blitzing.

SERVES 4–6
PREP: 35 MINUTES, PLUS MARINATING
COOK: 15 MINUTES

1 x 700g (1½lb) bavette steak

1 tsp hot smoked paprika

2 tsp dried Mexican (or standard) oregano

1 tsp chipotle or standard chilli flakes

1 garlic clove, crushed

4 tbsp olive oil

12 x 15cm (6in) soft corn tortillas, homemade (page 16) or shop-bought

Vine-Ripened Tomato Salsa (page 94), to serve

Flesh of 2 medium avocados, scooped into nuggets

FOR THE GREEN SAUCE

30g (1oz/2 tbsp) pine nuts or blanched almonds

1 small bunch of coriander (cilantro), plus extra leaves to serve

½ small bunch of parsley

1 fat garlic clove, peeled

120ml (4fl oz/½ cup) extra-virgin olive oil

Juice of 1 lime

A pinch of caster (superfine) sugar

Salt and black pepper

1. Place the steak in a large dish. Mix together the paprika, oregano, chilli flakes, garlic and olive oil, then rub the steak generously with the mixture and set aside, covered, in the fridge to marinate for 1–2 hours.

2. Toast the pine nuts or almonds in a small pan over a low heat for about 5 minutes or until lightly golden.

3. Place the coriander, parsley, garlic and toasted nuts into the small bowl of a food processor, along with the olive oil, and whizz until semi-chunky in consistency. Transfer to a bowl, stir through the lime juice and sugar, season generously with salt and pepper and set aside.

4. Heat a ridged griddle pan or non-stick frying pan (skillet) over a high heat until almost at smoking point. Add the marinated beef to the pan, season generously with salt and pepper and cook on each side for 3–4 minutes, depending on the thickness of the meat, for a medium-rare steak. Remove from the pan and allow to rest on a chopping board for 15 minutes, covered in foil.

5. Warm the tortillas through in a small dry frying pan, keeping a stack warm, wrapped in foil, in a low oven while you heat the rest. Cut the steak into slices about 1cm (½in) thick and arrange on top of each tortilla with a drizzle of the green sauce, a little of the salsa and some avocado nuggets. Finish with a few torn coriander leaves.

2

NACHOS

DEEP-FRIED TORTILLA CHIPS

All nacho recipes are based on the tortilla chip. Deep-frying tortillas is the traditional way to get a crisp and bubbly texture. They're so easy to make and will last for 2 days in an airtight container.

SERVES 4–6
PREP: 5 MINUTES
COOK: 10 MINUTES

16 x 20cm (8in) soft corn tortillas
1 litre (1¾ pints/4¼ cups) vegetable oil
Salt

1. Use a sharp knife to cut each tortilla into 6–8 triangles, like a pizza. Heat the oil in a deep-fryer, or in a large, deep heavy-based saucepan filled no more than two-thirds full, until the oil reaches 190°C (375°F) on a cooking thermometer. Alternatively, drop in a small cube of bread to check that the oil is hot enough; it should turn golden brown within 10 seconds.

2. Deep-fry the tortillas in the hot oil in 3–4 batches, cooking each batch for 30–40 seconds. Don't be tempted to let them get too dark-coloured – a light golden brown should be enough, and they will harden up as they cool. Remove with the slotted spoon and drain on kitchen paper (paper towels) before sprinkling with salt. Leave to cool down a little before eating.

EASY BAKED TORTILLA CHIPS

Baked tortilla chips are a little easier to make as well as being healthier than deep-fried ones. All you need is a pack of tortillas, some sunflower oil and a piping-hot oven! Use these to dip into guacamole (page 102), pile with toppings or scrunch up and scatter on top of soup instead of croutons.

SERVES 4–6
PREP: 5 MINUTES
COOK: 15–20 MINUTES

12 x 20cm (8in) soft corn tortillas

3 tbsp sunflower oil

½ tsp sweet smoked paprika (optional)

Salt

1. Preheat the oven to 200°C (180°C fan)/400°F/gas 6 and line 2–3 baking trays (cookie sheets) with foil.

2. Use a sharp knife to cut each tortilla into 6–8 triangles, like a pizza. Brush the triangles on each side with the sunflower oil and spread out on the prepared baking trays, making sure they form a single layer. Sprinkle over the paprika (if using), then bake in the oven, one tray at a time, for 5–6 minutes or until golden and bubbly.

3. Remove from the oven, sprinkle with salt and allow to cool almost entirely before eating.

ULTIMATE CLASSIC NACHOS

Everybody loves a mound of salty tortilla chips topped with molten cheese, salsa, guacamole, cool soured cream and crunchy pickles. This version uses homemade toppings (it's SO worth it!), but if you're feeling lazy just omit them for good-quality shop-bought varieties. Don't miss out a topping, though; all are equally important in creating the ultimate nachos!

SERVES 4–6
PREP: 15 MINUTES
COOK: 5 MINUTES

Tortilla chips: 1 x homemade (pages
    42–43) or 2 x 200g bags shop-bought

½ x 400g can black beans, drained
    and rinsed

1 tbsp olive oil

120g (4½oz) mature Cheddar, grated

120g (4½oz/generous 1 cup) grated
    mozzarella

1 handful of sliced fresh or Easy
    Pickled Jalapeños (page 106), drained

Leaves of ½ small bunch of coriander
    (cilantro)

Salt and black pepper

TO SERVE

Guacamole (page 102)

Vine-Ripened Tomato Salsa (page 94)

Soured cream

1. Preheat the grill (broiler) to high. Spread the tortilla chips out in a large baking tray (cookie sheet) or ovenproof dish and set aside.

2. Place the beans and olive oil in a small saucepan set over a low heat and gently mash with a potato masher until smooth and warmed through. Season to taste with salt and pepper.

3. Mix the two cheeses together and sprinkle on top of the tortilla chips. Cook under the grill for 2–3 minutes or until the cheese is golden and bubbling. Be careful not to let it catch or burn under the grill.

4. Dollop mounds of the guacamole, salsa and soured cream onto your nachos as well as the warmed black beans. Finish with the jalapeños and a handful of peppery coriander and then pull the gooey nachos apart!

NACHO BRUNCH BOWLS

Ditch your usual weekend fry-up for bowls filled with tortillas, homemade baked beans, runny fried eggs and crispy chorizo. Serve with a Green Agua Fresca (page 132) to wash down these delicious breakfast bundles! Perfect on those slightly blurry hungover Sunday mornings …

SERVES 4
PREP: I5 MINUTES
COOK: 35–40 MINUTES

3 tbsp olive oil

1 small red onion, sliced

2 small garlic cloves, crushed

2 tsp sweet smoked paprika

1 x 400g can chopped tomatoes

4 tsp Cholula or other chilli sauce

4 tbsp tomato ketchup

2 x 400g cans butterbeans, drained
and rinsed

150g (5oz) chorizo ring, thickly sliced

150g (5oz) mixed mushrooms, sliced

4 large free-range eggs

4 handfuls of homemade (pages 42–43)
or shop-bought tortilla chips

Salt and black pepper

Guacamole (page 102), to serve

1. Heat 1 tablespoon of the olive oil in a large frying pan (skillet) over a medium heat. Add the onion and fry for 10 minutes or until softened and turning golden brown. Stir through the garlic and paprika and cook for a further minute. Add the tomatoes, Cholula sauce, ketchup and butterbeans, then raise the heat and leave to bubble for 10 minutes. Season to taste with salt and pepper and keep warm over a low heat.

2. Place another tablespoon of oil in a second frying pan set over a medium heat and add the chorizo. Fry for 5–6 minutes or until brown and blistered, then remove from the pan with a slotted spoon and set aside. Add the mushrooms and fry in the chorizo oil for 6–7 minutes or until turning golden brown.

3. Place the remaining oil in a clean frying pan over a medium heat. Crack the eggs into the pan and fry until the yolks are just set but still runny and the whites are crispy around the edges.

4. Take four bowls and fill with the beans, then nestle some tortilla chips around the edges and top each bowl with a fried egg, the fried chorizo, mushrooms and a spoonful of guacamole. Season with pepper and use the tortillas to scoop up your brunch.

SPICED MANGO CHUTNEY AND CHILLI CHEESE NACHOS

Elements from the Indian pickle tray have been piled on top of these Asian-inspired nachos! Crunchy cool cucumber, spring onion and red chilli are paired with a gooey green chilli-cheese mix and blobs of sweet mango chutney. Ditch your Friday-night takeaway and curl up on the sofa with this Mexicana/Indian mash-up of nachos instead.

SERVES 4–6
PREP: 20 MINUTES
COOK: 5 MINUTES

1 heaped tsp cumin seeds

3 medium-sized plum tomatoes, deseeded finely chopped

3 spring onions (scallions), finely sliced

½ cucumber, deseeded and finely diced

Leaves of ½ small bunch of coriander (cilantro), roughly chopped

80g (3oz/⅓ cup) natural Greek yoghurt

Leaves of ½ small bunch of mint, roughly chopped

120g (4½oz) mature Cheddar, grated

120g (4½oz/generous 1 cup) grated mozzarella

1 medium fresh green chilli, deseeded and finely chopped

Tortilla chips: 1 x homemade (pages 42–43) or 2 x 200g bags shop-bought

4–5 tbsp mango chutney

1 fresh red chilli, finely sliced (optional)

1 tsp nigella seeds

Salt and black pepper

1. Lightly toast the cumin seeds in a small pan over a low heat for 2–3 minutes until they begin to pop and smell aromatic.

2. In a large bowl, combine the tomatoes, spring onions, cucumber and chopped coriander. Season to taste with salt.

3. In a separate bowl, stir together the yoghurt and chopped mint and season with salt and pepper. Toss the two cheeses together with the chopped green chilli and the toasted cumin seeds.

4. Preheat the grill (broiler) to high. Spread the tortilla chips out on a baking tray (cookie sheet) or in an ovenproof dish. Cover with mounds of the cheese and pop under the grill to cook for 1–2 minutes or until the cheese is golden and bubbling. Finish the nachos with the tomato and spring onion salad, the minted yoghurt and blobs of the mango chutney. Sprinkle over the chopped red chilli (if using) and nigella seeds. Alternatively, you can serve these nachos with the chutneys in pots on the side to dip into.

BARBECUE JACKFRUIT AND RAINBOW SLAW NACHOS

Jackfruit is a great sustainable replacement for meat, especially when pepped up with spices and smoky barbecue sauce! Its texture will fool you in to thinking you're eating pulled pork. The canned version is easy to get hold of online and in specialist supermarkets or world-food shops, but make sure you use the variety in water rather than salty brine for this recipe.

SERVES 4
PREP: 20 MINUTES
COOK: 25–30 MINUTES

2 x 400g cans jackfruit in water, drained and rinsed

2 tbsp maple syrup or (soft light) brown sugar

2 tsp sweet smoked paprika

1 tsp medium chilli powder

1 tsp ground coriander

½ tsp freshly ground black pepper

1 fat garlic clove, finely grated

1 tbsp sunflower or rapeseed oil

90ml (3fl oz/⅓ cup) good-quality barbecue sauce

3 tsp chipotle chilli paste

130ml (4½fl oz/generous ½ cup) water

Tortilla chips: 1 x homemade (pages 42–43) or 2 x 200g bags shop-bought

Guacamole (page 102), to serve

FOR THE SLAW

1 small carrot, cut into thin matchsticks

1 small red (bell) pepper, deseeded and thinly sliced

¼ large red cabbage, shredded

2 spring onions (scallions), finely sliced

½ small bunch of coriander (cilantro), finely chopped

Juice of 1 large lime

Salt and black pepper

1. Pat the jackfruit dry with kitchen paper (paper towels). To prepare, cut the core out and, using a fork, roughly shred the rest into a bowl. Add the sugar, paprika, chilli powder, ground coriander, black pepper and grated garlic to the bowl and mix until the jackfruit is well covered. Set aside.

2. To make the slaw, mix the carrot, red pepper, cabbage, spring onion and chopped coriander in a large bowl. Toss in the lime juice and season well with salt and pepper.

3. Heat the oil in a large non-stick pan (with a lid). Add the shredded jackfruit and fry for 5–6 minutes, stirring occasionally, until it has deepened in colour. Stir though the barbecue sauce, chipotle chilli paste and water. Turn the heat down to low and cover the pan with the lid. Allow the jackfruit to cook for 20 minutes to tenderise and develop flavour. Season with salt.

4. Arrange the tortilla chips on a large serving plate and top with the warm barbecue jackfruit, bundles of the slaw and spoonfuls of the creamy guacamole.

SLOW-COOKED SHORT RIB NACHOS

Melt-in-the-mouth short ribs are used in this rich, hearty dish for ultimate Friday night indulgence. Leave them to cook slowly in the pot during the day and enjoy them with friends in the evening piled onto nachos and with a few ice-cold Mexican beers!

SERVES 6 AS A STARTER AND 8 AS PART OF A WIDER SHARING TABLE
PREP: 30 MINUTES
COOK: 3½–4 HOURS

Olive oil, for frying

1.3kg (2¾lb) beef short ribs

1 large onion, finely chopped

2 fat garlic cloves, crushed

1 tsp hot smoked paprika

2 tsp ground cumin

2 tsp coriander seeds, lightly crushed

3 bay leaves

1 cinnamon stick

1 dried chipotle chilli or 1 tbsp chipotle chilli paste

1 x 400g can chopped tomatoes

2 tbsp tomato purée

500ml (18fl oz/2 cups) beef stock

1 tbsp (soft dark) brown sugar

2 small squares of dark chocolate (minimum 70 per cent cocoa solids)

Tortilla chips: 1 x homemade (pages 42–43) or 2 x 200g bags shop-bought

150g (5oz) Taleggio or Cheddar, cubed

1 handful of Easy Pickled Jalapeños (page 106), drained

1 large fresh red chilli, sliced

Handful of coriander (cilantro), torn

Salt and black pepper

TO SERVE

Guacamole (page 102); Soured cream; Lime wedges

1. Heat 1 tablespoon of olive oil in a large, heavy-based saucepan (with a lid) over a high heat. Season the ribs with salt and pepper and fry, in batches, on each side for 3–5 minutes or until dark brown. Set the ribs aside on a plate.

2. Pour another tablespoon of oil into the same pan, then add the onion and a pinch of salt. Fry over a medium heat for 8–10 minutes or until softened. Add the garlic and cook for 1 minute. Stir though the paprika, cumin and crushed coriander seeds and cook for a further 2 minutes.

3. Add the bay leaves, cinnamon stick, chipotle chilli/paste, canned tomatoes, tomato purée, stock and sugar and bring to the boil. Reduce the heat to a simmer and return the browned ribs to the pan. Cover and cook on a low heat for 3–3½ hours or until the meat is falling off the bone. Check the pan every now and then, adding a splash of water if needed.

4. Remove the ribs from the sauce and use a fork to pull the meat from the bones. Discard the bones and return the meat to the pan. If the sauce looks a little thin, let it bubble over a medium heat for 10–15 minutes until thickened. Remove the bay leaves, cinnamon stick and chipotle chilli (if using). Season to taste with salt and pepper and stir through the chocolate.

5. Preheat the grill (broiler) to medium. Spread the tortilla chips out on a baking tray (cookie sheet) or in an ovenproof dish. Top with the meat, using it all if you fancy, or saving some for later. Scatter over the cheese and pop under the grill to cook for 3–4 minutes or until molten and bubbling.

6. Top with some guacamole and soured cream, along with the pickles, sliced chilli and torn coriander leaves. Serve with lime wedges and pass the napkins around!

VEGGIE CHILLI WITH CHIPOTLES IN ADOBO

A chilli doesn't need to be meat-based. This veggie recipe is bulked out with sweet peppers and mixed beans. The smoky, spicy tones come from a humble can of chipotles in adobo. These plump chipotle chillies in a rich tomato sauce are whizzed up and stirred though the bubbling mixture. You can get hold of chipotles in adobo sauce online or in Mexican food shops. If you don't manage to find them, just swirl through two or three tablespoons of chipotle chilli paste instead.

SERVES 4 AS MAIN AND 6 AS STARTER
PREP: 20 MINUTES
COOK: 40 MINUTES

3 tbsp olive oil

1 red onion, chopped

1 red (bell) pepper, deseeded and sliced

1 yellow (bell) pepper, deseeded and sliced

1 small bunch of coriander (cilantro),
    stalks chopped and leaves reserved

2 garlic cloves, crushed

½ tsp hot smoked paprika

2 tsp ground cumin

2 tsp ground coriander

1 x 200g can chipotles in adobo sauce

1 x 400g can kidney beans, rinsed

1 x 400g can black-eyed beans, rinsed

1 x 400g can chopped tomatoes

2 tbsp (soft light) brown sugar

50g (2oz) mature Cheddar, grated

50g (2oz/½ cup) grated mozzarella

3 spring onions (scallions), finely sliced

Tortilla chips: 1 x homemade (pages
    42–43) or 2 x 200g bags shop-bought

Salt and black pepper

TO SERVE

Guacamole (page 102); Soured cream;
    Pico de Gallo Salsa (page 95)
    (optional); Lime wedges

1. Heat the olive oil in a large, deep frying pan (skillet) or wide, heavy-based saucepan. Add the onion, along with a pinch of salt, and fry over a low heat for 7 minutes. Add the red and yellow peppers and fry for a further 5 minutes. Stir through the chopped coriander stalks with the garlic, paprika, cumin and ground coriander and cook for 3 more minutes.

2. Blitz the tinned chipotles to a smooth paste in a food processor, or finely chop by hand. Stir the chipotles through the vegetables, along with the beans, tomatoes and sugar. Bring to the boil, then reduce to a simmer and cook, uncovered, for 20 minutes.

3. Preheat the grill (broiler) to medium. Sprinkle the cheese directly over the chilli and place under the grill to cook for 3–4 minutes or until the cheese is molten and golden brown. Top with the reserved coriander leaves and the spring onions and serve with some guacamole, soured cream, salsa and lime wedges, as well as a big bowl of salty tortilla chips to scoop it up!

CHARRED VEGETABLE AND RICOTTA NACHOS

Charred vegetables and creamy ricotta are piled onto crisp tortillas in this summer recipe. For extra flavour, try barbecuing your veg instead of griddling them. This is a perfect veg-centric dish for those who fancy an alternative to bean-based vegetarian nachos.

SERVES 4–6
PREP: 15 MINUTES
COOK: 20 MINUTES

250g (9oz) mixed Romano or standard (bell) peppers, large and small, halved and deseeded

1 large red onion, cut into wedges

3 tsp hot smoked paprika

2 tsp ground coriander

3 tbsp olive oil

220g (7½oz) vine-ripened cherry tomatoes

150g (5oz/⅔ cup) ricotta

50g (2oz/¼ cup) natural Greek yoghurt

Leaves of ½ bunch of dill, finely chopped, plus extra sprigs to garnish

Tortilla chips: 1 x homemade (pages 42–43) or 2 x 200g bags shop-bought

1 fresh green chilli, sliced

Salt and black pepper

1. Preheat the oven to 180°C (160°C fan)/350°F/gas 4.

2. Slice any larger peppers and place in a bowl with the smaller pepper halves and the onion wedges. Add the paprika, ground coriander and 1 tablespoon of the olive oil, then season to taste with salt and pepper.

3. Place the tomatoes, still on the vine, on a baking tray (cookie sheet) and drizzle with 1 tablespoon of the olive oil. Season with salt and pepper and roast in the oven for 10 minutes.

4. Spoon the ricotta into a bowl, add the yoghurt and mix together until smooth. Stir through the chopped dill and season to taste with salt and pepper.

5. Heat a ridged griddle pan or heavy-based frying pan (skillet) over a high heat until almost at smoking point. In batches, char the peppers and onions on each side for 3–4 minutes or until softened and blackened. Set aside.

6. Pile the tortilla chips into a serving bowl. Top with the charred veg and roasted tomatoes and drizzle with the remaining olive oil. Finish with spoonfuls of the ricotta mixture, green chilli and a few extra sprigs of dill.

VEGAN SWEET POTATO NACHOS WITH CRISPY ONIONS

With everyone having some vegan friends these days, an easy plant-based recipe will come in handy for most of us at some point. These vegan nachos are great for everyone to share. The spiced nuggets of sweet potato, creamy chipotle cashew cream and crispy deep-fried onions are an absolute treat – your non-vegan friends won't even know!

SERVES 4–6
PREP: 35 MINUTES
COOK: 25–30 MINUTES

500g (1lb 2oz) sweet potatoes, peeled and cut into 1cm (½in) cubes

1 tbsp olive oil

1 tsp ground cumin

1 tsp ground coriander

½ tsp hot chilli powder

100g (3½oz/⅔ cup) unsalted cashew nuts

140ml (5fl oz/⅔ cup) cashew or any other nut milk

2–3 tsp chipotle chilli paste

300ml (10fl oz/1¼ cups) sunflower oil

1 whole large red onion, finely sliced into thin rounds

Tortilla chips: 1 x homemade (pages 42–43) or 2 x 200g bags shop-bought

1–2 limes, quartered

Fine salt and black pepper

Pico de Gallo Salsa (page 95), to serve

1. Preheat the oven to 200°C (180°C fan)/400°F/gas 6.

2. Place the sweet potato on a baking tray (cookie sheet), add the oil, cumin, coriander and chilli powder and toss together before arranging the sweet potato cubes in a single layer. Season with salt and pepper and roast in the oven for 20–25 minutes or until tender.

3. Meanwhile, place the cashew nuts in a bowl of boiling water and leave to soak for 15 minutes. Drain and place in a blender or the small bowl of a food processor. Add the nut milk, 2 teaspoons of the chipotle chilli paste and ½ teaspoon of salt and blitz until completely smooth. Taste the mixture: if you like it a little spicier, add more of the chipotle paste. Spoon into a bowl and set aside.

4. Line a baking tray with kitchen paper (paper towels). Pour the sunflower oil into a large, deep heavy-based saucepan and set over a medium heat. After around 10 minutes, bubbles should begin to rise to the surface; this means the oil is hot enough to fry in. In batches, fry the onions in the hot oil for 2–3 minutes or until just beginning to darken and curl up. Remove with a slotted spoon and drain on the kitchen paper, then sprinkle over a little salt to keep them crisp.

5. Pile the tortilla chips onto a serving plate and top with the roasted sweet potato, drizzle over the cashew cream and spoon over the salsa. Finish with bundles of the crispy onions and squeeze over the limes to serve!

GREEK NACHOS WITH TOMATO AND CUCUMBER SALSA

Think Greek salad, deconstructed and piled onto crisp tortilla chips. This slightly lighter version of nachos is perfect on a hot summer day to enjoy with pals. Share between two for lunch or among four as a pre-dinner snack.

SERVES 2–4
PREP: 15 MINUTES
COOK: 3 MINUTES

1 tsp coriander seeds

Tortilla chips: ½ quantity of homemade (pages 42–43) or 1 x 200g bag shop-bought

120g (4½oz) good-quality Greek feta, sliced or crumbled

Leaves of ½ bunch of oregano, torn

FOR THE TOMATO AND CUCUMBER SALSA

150g (5oz) ripe cherry tomatoes, halved

2 tbsp extra-virgin olive oil, plus extra for drizzling

Leaves of ½ small bunch of mint, finely chopped

Leaves of 1 small bunch of dill, finely chopped

½ small red onion, finely sliced

3 baby cucumbers, sliced

40g (1½oz/¼ cup) pitted Kalamata olives

Zest and juice of ½ small lemon

Salt and black pepper

1. In a bowl, toss together the cherry tomatoes, olive oil, mint, dill, red onion, cucumber and olives. Season to taste with salt and pepper, bearing in mind that the olives and feta are already salty, and add the lemon zest and juice.

2. Lightly toast the coriander seeds in a small pan over a low heat for 2–3 minutes until they begin to pop and smell aromatic. Crush lightly using a pestle and mortar or the back of a knife.

3. Arrange the tortilla chips in a large serving bowl. Top with the tomato and cucumber salsa, followed by the feta, toasted coriander seeds and torn oregano leaves. Finish with a drizzle of olive oil, if you like.

SKILLET SMOKY ANCHO MEATBALL NACHOS

These indulgent nachos are topped with delicious pork meatballs, a rich ancho chilli and tomato sauce and super-gooey fontina cheese. Make these for your partner or friends for a relaxed meal at the weekend. They are easier than you think to throw together and are guaranteed to impress!

SERVES 4–6
PREP: 25 MINUTES
COOK: 50–55 MINUTES

400g (14oz/2 cups) minced pork

½ tsp chilli flakes

2 tsp Mexican (or standard) dried oregano

100g (3½oz/3½ cups) fresh white breadcrumbs

1 small bunch of parsley, finely chopped, plus extra to serve (optional)

1 large free-range egg yolk

3 tbsp olive oil

1 onion, finely chopped

2 garlic cloves, crushed

2 tsp sweet smoked paprika

¼ tsp hot chilli powder

1 x 400g can chopped tomatoes

1 dried ancho chilli or 1 tbsp ancho paste

2 bay leaves

100ml (3½fl oz/½ cup) water

2 tbsp (soft light) brown sugar

½ tbsp balsamic vinegar

2 tbsp whole milk

Tortilla chips: 1 x homemade (pages 42–43) or 1 x 200g bag shop-bought

100g (3½oz) fontina or Taleggio cheese, cubed, or grated mozzarella

Salt and black pepper

Finely chopped parsley and Easy Pickled Jalapeños (page 106), to serve (optional)

1. Place the minced pork in a large bowl with the chilli flakes, oregano, breadcrumbs, parsley and egg yolk and season with salt and pepper. Mix everything together with your hands for 5 minutes: squishing the meat for a good length of time gives nice, firmer-textured meatballs when cooked. Divide the mixture into 12 meatballs and chill in the fridge until ready to use.

2. In a large, heavy-based saucepan, heat 2 tablespoons of the olive oil over a medium heat. Add the onion, along with a good pinch of salt, and fry for 7–10 minutes until softened and turning translucent. Add the garlic, paprika and chilli powder and cook for a further minute.

3. Tip in the tomatoes, ancho chilli or ancho paste, bay leaves and water. Stir through the sugar and vinegar and bring the mixture to the boil. Reduce the heat and simmer for 25 minutes, uncovered, or until thickened and reduced by a third. Stir through the milk and season to taste with salt and pepper.

4. Preheat the oven to 180°C (160°C fan)/350°F/gas 4.

5. Heat the remaining oil in a non-stick frying pan (skillet) over a medium heat and add the meatballs. Fry for 5–7 minutes until evenly browned and beginning to cook through, then transfer to an ovenproof dish and pop in the oven to bake for a further 10–12 minutes or until cooked through.

6. Preheat the grill (broiler) to medium. Pile the tortilla chips into an ovenproof dish or roasting pan. Top with the meatballs, tomato sauce and cheese. Place under the grill to cook for 2–3 minutes or until the cheese is molten. Sprinkle over some extra parsley or pickled jalapeños and then pull the gooey meatball nachos apart!

SMOKY CRISPY CHICKEN AND CHARRED CORN NACHOS

Ideal for sharing with friends – ditch the fiddly forks and use the nachos to scoop up the smoky Mexican flavours! The crispy chicken is achieved by cooking the skin separately. If you don't have time, simply discard the skin and continue cooking the meat as per recipe.

SERVES 4–6
PREP: 35 MINUTES
COOK: 1¼ HOURS

1 large dried chipotle chilli

40g (1½oz/scant ¼ cup) unsalted butter, softened

¼ tsp ground coriander

¼ tsp ground cumin

½ tsp sweet smoked paprika

4 chicken thighs, skin on and bone in

2 large corn on the cob

1 x 400g can black beans, drained and rinsed

Flesh of 1 medium-sized ripe avocado, cubed

3 medium-sized ripe tomatoes, diced

2 spring onions (scallions), finely sliced

Zest and juice of 2 limes

1 small bunch of coriander (cilantro), roughly chopped

30g (1oz/⅛ cup) soured cream

70ml (3fl oz/⅓ cup) buttermilk

2 tbsp finely snipped chives

Tortilla chips: 1 x homemade (pages 42–43) or 2 x 200g bags shop-bought

Salt and black pepper

1. Preheat the oven to 200°C (180°C fan)/400°F/gas 6 and line a flat baking tray (cookie sheet) with baking parchment.

2. Soak the dried chilli in boiling water for 10 minutes. Remove the seeds and finely chop the flesh, then mash together with the softened butter and a good pinch of salt. Set aside.

3. In a small bowl, combine the ground coriander, cumin and paprika. Remove the skin from the chicken and place on the prepared baking tray. Rub with the spices and season generously. Place another flat baking tray on top to press the skin down, and cook in the oven for 25–30 minutes or until crispy. Leave to cool before breaking into shards.

4. Reduce the oven temperature to 180°C (160°C fan)/350°F/gas 4. Rub the chicken thighs with the chilli butter and place in a medium-sized baking dish. Cover with foil and bake in the oven for 30–35 minutes or until cooked through. Take out of the oven and set aside until cool. Once cooled, remove the chicken from the bone and shred into strips.

5. Bring a large saucepan of water to the boil, add the corn and cook for 5 minutes, then drain. Heat a ridged griddle pan or heavy-based frying pan (skillet) over a high heat until almost at smoking point. Add the corn and cook for 8–10 minutes, turning every now and again. Set aside to cool, then use a sharp knife to slice off kernels in chunks.

6. Mix together the corn kernels, black beans, avocado, tomatoes and spring onion. Stir through the lime zest and juice and half the chopped coriander, and season. In a separate bowl, mix together the soured cream, buttermilk and chives and season.

7. Pile the tortilla chips into a large serving bowl. Top with the corn and bean mixture, shredded chicken and crispy skin. Drizzle over the dressing and top with the remaining coriander.

MIDDLE EASTERN LAMB NACHOS

Turkish flatbreads have had a revamp in this Middle Eastern-style nacho mash-up. Ras el hanout, the spice mixture used for flavouring the dish, is north African in origin and includes cardamom, cumin, nutmeg and dried rose petals. You can buy it in most supermarkets in the world food or spice section.

SERVES 4
PREP: 15 MINUTES
COOK: 25 MINUTES

25g (1oz/2 tbsp) pine nuts

½ tbsp olive oil

1 tbsp unsalted butter

1 banana shallot, sliced

350g (12oz/1½ cups) minced lamb

3 tsp ras el hanout

1 fat garlic clove, grated

Leaves of ½ small bunch of parsley, roughly chopped

Leaves of ½ small bunch of dill, chopped

Juice of ½ lemon

100g (3½oz/⅓ cup) natural yoghurt

1 tbsp tahini

50ml (2fl oz/¼ cup) water

Tortilla chips: ½ x homemade (pages 42–43) or 1 x 200g bag shop-bought

1 small handful of pomegranate seeds

Salt and black pepper

1. Toast the pine nuts in a small pan over a low heat for about 5 minutes or until lightly golden, then set aside.

2. Heat the oil and butter together in a non-stick pan over a medium heat. Add the shallot and fry for 7–10 minutes or until softened and beginning to caramelise and turn golden brown.

3. Add the mince to the pan, breaking it up with a wooden spoon, and fry for 10 minutes or until browned and turning crispy. Stir in the ras el hanout and garlic and cook for a final minute.

4. Remove from the heat and stir through most of the toasted pine nuts and parsley, half the dill and all the lemon juice. Season to taste with salt and pepper and keep warm over a very low heat.

5. Mix together the yoghurt and tahini, along with the water, to create a creamy mixture to drizzle.

6. Spread the tortillas out on a serving plate and top with the warm spiced mince. Drizzle over the tahini dressing and scatter with the pomegranate seeds and the remaining pine nuts and parsley.

CHORIZO AND PRAWN TOPPED NACHOS

The moreish combination of chorizo and prawns is the star of this nacho recipe. Make a batch of your own tortillas, top each one with a little of the mixture and serve to guests as a pre-dinner snackette!

SERVES 4–6
PREP: 15 MINUTES
COOK: 7 MINUTES

180g (6oz) peeled raw king prawns (jumbo shrimp)

160g (5½oz) cooking chorizo, skin removed

1 tbsp olive oil

3 spring onions (scallions), finely chopped

½ small bunch of coriander (cilantro), very finely chopped

Tortilla chips: ½ x homemade (pages 42–43) or 1 x 200g bag shop-bought

3 limes, quartered

Black pepper

1. Very finely chop the prawns until almost minced, then transfer to a bowl. Very finely chop the chorizo and combine with the prawns in the bowl. Season the mixture with a little black pepper.

2. Heat the olive oil in a non-stick pan over a medium-high heat. Add the chorizo and prawn mixture and fry for about 7 minutes, breaking it up with the back of a wooden spoon and cooking until any liquid released from the prawns has evaporated.

3. Combine the spring onions and coriander in another bowl. You can either top each tortilla chip with a spoonful of the chorizo mixture and a sprinkling of the coriander or serve the mixture in a hot pan with the nachos on the side to scoop up the chorizo and prawns. Either way, make sure there are plenty of limes wedges on hand to cut through the rich flavours.

CEVICHE

Ceviche is a dish of raw cubed fish doused in lemon or lime juice and left to marinate. The acid in the citrus fruit almost cooks the outside of the fish, giving the flesh a tender, meaty texture. Make sure you use top-quality fish for this one. It's best served with cantina chips, if you can get hold of them, or a batch of the Deep-Fried Tortilla Chips on page 42.

SERVES 2–4
PREP: 15 MINUTES, PLUS MARINATING

2 x 150g (5oz) skinless and boneless sea bass fillets

3 limes: juice of 3 and zest of 1

1 spring onion (scallion), finely sliced

1 large fresh red chilli, deseeded and finely chopped

Stalks of ½ small bunch of coriander (cilantro), finely chopped

1 small handful of garlic chives, snipped, or salad cress (optional)

Tortilla chips: ½ x homemade (pages 42–43) or 1 x 200g bag shop-bought

Sea salt

1. Make sure there are no bones left in the fish, then cut each fillet up into 1cm (½in) cubes. Place in a bowl with the lime juice and zest, sliced spring onion, chopped chilli and coriander. Cover and place in the fridge to marinate for 1½–2 hours.

2. Stir ½ teaspoon of salt through the marinated ceviche. Spoon onto a serving plate and serve topped with the garlic chives or salad cress. Finish with a little extra pinch of salt and scoop up using the crispy tortillas.

3

SNACKS

THREE RECIPES FOR LITTLE TOSTADAS

A tostada is little disc of tortilla that's deep-fried until golden brown and crisp and then topped with other ingredients. Perfect to hand around at parties for people to just pick up and pop into their mouths. Cut the discs close together to get as many as possible out of one tortilla. And try making all three recipes to mix and match on a sharing platter.

TUNA AND SESAME TOSTADAS

A little Asian twist on a Mexican dish. Tiny pieces of tuna are tossed in sesame oil and sesame seeds, along with cubed avocado, to make seriously moreish bites. Choose a slightly under-ripe avocado for this dish as it will be easier to cut into little cubes, and be sure you ask your fishmonger for tuna that is sushi-grade and therefore suitable for eating sashimi-style.

MAKES 20 LITTLE TOSTADAS
PREP: 25 MINUTES, PLUS COOLING
COOK: 5 MINUTES

4–5 x 20cm (8in) soft corn tortillas

1.5 litres (2½ pints/6 cups) sunflower oil

300g (11oz) sushi-grade tuna steaks, cut into 1cm (½in) cubes

3 tbsp sesame oil

Stalks of 1 small bunch of coriander (cilantro), finely chopped

1 small fresh red chilli, deseeded and finely chopped

1 heaped tsp fine salt

Flesh of ½ large avocado, finely cubed

1 tsp black or white sesame seeds, plus extra to serve

Lime wedges, to serve

You will also need a 7cm (2¾in) pastry cutter

1. Use the pastry cutter to cut each tortilla into 4–5 discs. Heat the sunflower oil in a deep-fryer, or in a large, deep heavy-based saucepan filled no more than two-thirds full, until the oil reaches 190°C (375°F) on a cooking thermometer. Alternatively, drop in a small cube of bread to check that the oil is hot enough; it should turn golden brown within 10 seconds.

2. Use a slotted spoon to lower the tortilla discs into the oil, about five at a time, and cook each batch for 30 seconds or until turning golden brown. Remove with the slotted spoon and place on a tray lined with kitchen paper (paper towels). Leave to cool down for 15 minutes.

3. Place the tuna in a bowl and stir through the sesame oil, coriander stalks, red chilli and salt. Gently fold through the avocado and sesame seeds.

4. Spoon a teaspoon of the tuna mixture on to each of the little tostadas. Finish with some extra sesame seeds and the lime wedges.

AVOCADO, POPPED BLACK BEAN AND RADISH TOSTADAS

Heating a pan until almost at smoking point and then adding the black beans makes them pop and crackle like little jumping beans! You're left with a slightly crispy exterior and a soft middle. These tostadas are topped with said beans, mashed avocado and a quick radish pickle. So easy – and they just so happen to be vegan too!

MAKES 20 LITTLE TOSTADAS
PREP: 30 MINUTES, PLUS COOLING
COOK: 5 MINUTES

4–5 x 20cm (8in) soft corn tortillas

1.5 litres (2½ pints/6 cups) sunflower oil

7 radishes, finely sliced

Zest and juice of 2 limes

½ x 400g can black beans, drained
  and rinsed

Flesh of 2 medium-sized ripe avocados

1 small fresh red chilli, deseeded and
  finely chopped

1 small handful of baby pea shoots or
  shredded coriander (cilantro)

Fine salt and black pepper

*You will also need a 7cm (2¾in) pastry
  cutter*

1. Use the pastry cutter to cut each tortilla into 4–5 discs. Heat the sunflower oil in a deep-fryer, or in a large, deep heavy-based saucepan filled no more than two-thirds full, until the oil reaches 190°C (375°F) on a cooking thermometer. Alternatively, drop in a small cube of bread to check that the oil is hot enough; it should turn golden brown within 10 seconds.

2. Use a slotted spoon to lower the tortilla discs into the oil, about five at a time, and cook each batch for 30 seconds or until turning golden brown. Remove with the slotted spoon and place on a tray lined with kitchen paper (paper towels). Leave to cool down for 15 minutes.

3. Place the sliced radish in a bowl and mix with half the lime zest and juice and ½ teaspoon of salt, and set aside for 10 minutes.

4. Meanwhile, pat the rinsed black beans dry with kitchen paper (paper towels). Heat a non-stick frying pan (skillet) over a high heat. Add the beans and dry-fry for 5–6 minutes or until popping and turning crisp. Season to taste with salt and pepper and set aside.

5. Place the avocado flesh in a bowl and mash with a fork until smooth, then stir though the remaining lime zest and juice and another ½ teaspoon of salt.

6. Top each tostada with a teaspoon each of avocado and popped beans and a few of the sliced radishes. Finish with some chilli slices and pea shoots or shredded coriander.

SMOKED SALMON AND SPRING ONION TOSTADAS

Just like those little salmon canapés you get at weddings or Christmas parties but way easier and more exciting! Mexican-style crema, a combo of soured cream and mayonnaise, is paired with smoked salmon, spring onion and punchy lime. Hand them round and be hostess with the mostest!

MAKES 20 LITTLE TOSTADAS
PREP: 15 MINUTES, PLUS COOLING
COOK: 5 MINUTES

4–5 x 20cm (8in) soft corn tortillas

1.5 litres (2½ pints/6 cups) sunflower oil

80g (3oz/⅓cup) soured cream

2 tbsp mayonnaise

130g (4½oz) smoked salmon
  slices, torn

3 spring onions (scallions), very
  finely sliced

2 tsp black or pink peppercorns,
  crushed

1 small handful of garlic chives,
  snipped (optional)

Lime wedges, to serve

*You will also need a 7cm (2¾in) pastry
  cutter*

1. Use the pastry cutter to cut each tortilla into 4–5 discs. Heat the sunflower oil in a deep-fryer, or in a large, deep heavy-based saucepan filled no more than two-thirds full, until the oil reaches 190°C (375°F) on a cooking thermometer. Alternatively, drop in a small cube of bread to check that the oil is hot enough; it should turn golden brown within 10 seconds.

2. Use a slotted spoon to lower the tortilla discs into the oil, about five at a time, and cook each batch for 30 seconds or until turning golden brown. Remove with the slotted spoon and place on a tray lined with kitchen paper (paper towels). Leave to cool down for 15 minutes.

3. In a bowl, combine the soured cream and mayonnaise.

4. Top each tostada with a teaspoon of crema, some smoked salmon and sliced spring onion. Finish with a sprinkling of crushed pepper, garlic chives and some lime wedges to squeeze over!

GRILLED CORN ON THE COB WITH CHILLI AND LIME BUTTER

Whipping together a flavoured butter can quickly transform the humble corn on the cob. In Mexico they top it with spiced butter, crumbled cheese and sometimes even a smear of mayonnaise. Char these golden husks on a griddle or throw on the barbecue in the summer and cook until blackened and smoky!

SERVES 4
PREP: 15 MINUTES
COOK: 15 MINUTES

80g (3oz/⅓ cup) unsalted butter, softened

1 tsp chipotle or standard chilli flakes

1 tsp sweet smoked paprika

Zest of 2 large limes

2 heaped tbsp finely grated Parmesan, plus extra to serve

4 large corn on the cob

30g (1oz) feta or queso fresco, crumbled

Leaves of ½ small bunch of coriander (cilantro), shredded

Salt

1. In a small bowl, mash together the softened butter with the chilli flakes, paprika, lime zest and Parmesan. Season generously with salt and set aside.

2. Bring a large saucepan of lightly salted water to the boil. Add the corn on the cob to the pan and simmer for 5 minutes or until tender. Drain in a colander set over the pan and allow to steam dry.

3. Heat a ridged griddle pan or non-stick frying pan (skillet) over a high heat until almost at smoking point. Add the corn to the pan and cook on each side for 5 minutes or until charred and blistered. Remove from the heat and liberally rub with the chilli butter.

4. Place on a serving plate, sprinkle with extra Parmesan and the crumbled feta or queso fresco and finish with the shredded coriander.

MEXICAN SPICED NUTS AND SEEDS

Roasting nuts with a few store cupboard spices is really easy and makes a great party snack. Mexican chipotle chilli flakes work really well on these nuts – try and get hold of them if you can. They're available online or in specialist Mexican shops.

MAKES 1 X 1 LITRE (1¾ PINT) JAR
PREP: 10 MINUTES, PLUS COOLING
COOK: 10 MINUTES

400g (14oz/3 cups) unsalted mixed
   nuts (such as pistachios, almonds,
   roasted peanuts and pecans)

50g (2oz/⅓ cup) pumpkin seeds

2 tbsp runny honey

30g (1oz/2 tbsp) unsalted butter,
   melted

3 tsp sweet smoked paprika

½ tsp hot smoked paprika

1 tsp ground cumin

4 tsp chipotle or standard chilli flakes

2 heaped tsp fine salt

1. Preheat the oven to 180°C (160°C fan)/350°F/gas 4.

2. Toss the nuts and seeds together and spread out on a large baking tray (cookie sheet) in a single layer. Drizzle over the honey and melted butter and place in the oven to roast for 10 minutes, tossing halfway through.

3. Meanwhile, dry-fry the paprika (sweet and hot), cumin and chilli flakes in a small pan.

4. Remove the nuts from the oven, tip into a bowl and toss in the toasted spice mixture and salt, then leave to cool down before piling into bowls. Alternatively, store in a clean sealed jar for up to 2 weeks.

WATERMELON WEDGES WITH LIME AND PINK PEPPERCORN SALT

In Mexico this refreshing combination is very popular; a pinch of salt helps to bring out the sweetness of the melon. Be brave and give this salty and sweet combo a try.

SERVES 6–8
PREP: 10 MINUTES

½ large or 1 small watermelon

1 tbsp sea salt flakes

1 tbsp caster (superfine) sugar

1 tsp pink peppercorns, crushed

Zest of 3 large limes

1. Slice the watermelon crossways into sections 2cm (¾in) thick and cut each section into triangular quarters. Set aside until ready to serve.

2. In a small bowl, mix together the salt, sugar, crushed peppercorns and lime zest. Serve the wedges of watermelon on a platter or serving plate with a pot of the sweet and salty mix to dip into.

CHICKEN AND CHIPOTLE AIOLI TORTAS

Along with salt beef bagels, grilled paninis and dainty cucumber sandwiches, Mexican tortas hold a firm place in the sandwich hall of fame. Sold regularly on the streets of Mexico, a hot torta consists traditionally of a toasted bun filled with refried beans, salad and cooked meat. You can swap the cooked chicken here for folded slices of mortadella, some charred chorizo or roasted vegetables, if you fancy!

SERVES 5
PREP: 15 MINUTES
COOK: 10–30 MINUTES

Flesh of 1 medium-sized ripe avocado

Juice of 1 lime

5 rashers (slices) of smoked
   streaky bacon

180g (6oz) cooked chicken, shredded

4 tbsp canned refried beans

1 x 270g long ciabatta loaf

1 tbsp olive oil

3–4 tbsp Chipotle Aioli (page 107)

Leaves of 1 small handful of coriander
   (cilantro), torn

2 medium-sized ripe tomatoes, sliced

1 Baby Gem lettuce, leaves separated

1 mild fresh green chilli, sliced
   (optional)

Salt and black pepper

Chilli jam or Fiery Habanero Chilli
   Sauce (page 101), to serve (optional)

1. Slice the avocado, sprinkle with the lime juice and set aside.

2. Preheat the grill (broiler) to high and line a flat baking tray (cookie sheet) with foil. Lay the bacon on the lined tray and grill for 5–6 minutes, turning over halfway, until crisp. Set aside.

3. Wrap the chicken in foil and warm through in the oven (preheated to 180°C (160°C fan)/350°F/gas 4) for 20–25 minutes, or keep it cold, if you prefer.

4. Gently warm the refried beans in a small saucepan over a medium heat for several minutes. Slice the ciabatta in half horizontally, rub the cut sides with the olive oil and toast under the grill on a medium heat until turning brown.

5. Spread the base of the loaf with the refried beans and the top with the chipotle aioli. Cover the beans with the sliced avocado, shredded chicken and crisp bacon and then top with the coriander, tomatoes, lettuce and chilli and season with salt and pepper. Sandwich together and slice into four. Crack open a cold soda and eat with a blob of chilli jam or habanero chilli sauce, if you're feeling brave.

SPICY BEEF BURRITO BITES

Roll up a few big burritos, slice up and eat as a snack or wrap up in paper for a picnic with friends. These delicious bites are easy to make and you can adjust the spiciness to your liking by adding less or more hot smoked paprika.

MAKES 16 SMALL BITES OR 4 LARGE BURRITOS
PREP: 25 MINUTES
COOK: 25 MINUTES

3 tbsp olive oil

1 onion, finely sliced

400g (14oz/scant 2 cups) lean minced beef

1 fat garlic clove, crushed

½ tsp ground cinnamon

1 tsp ground coriander

1 tsp sweet smoked paprika

1 tsp hot smoked paprika

3 spring onions (scallions), thinly sliced

200g (7oz) cherry tomatoes, quartered

1 small bunch of coriander (cilantro), roughly chopped

Juice of 2 limes

Flesh of 1 medium-sized avocado, diced

100g (3½oz/scant ½ cup) soured cream

2 tbsp mayonnaise

1 tbsp chipotle chilli paste

1 x 200g pouch of cooked basmati rice

4 large seeded or standard flour tortillas

2 Little Gem lettuces, leaves separated and shredded

70g (2½oz) medium Cheddar, grated (optional)

Salt and black pepper

Chilli sauce, to serve

1. Heat the olive oil in a medium frying pan (skillet) over a medium heat. Add the sliced onion, along with a pinch of salt, and fry for 10 minutes or until beginning to soften and turn golden brown. Add the minced beef, raise the heat and fry for 7 minutes, breaking up the meat with a wooden spoon and cooking until browned. Stir through the garlic, cinnamon, ground coriander, paprika (sweet and hot) and cook for a further 3 minutes. Remove from the heat and set aside.

2. Place the spring onions, tomatoes and chopped coriander in a bowl and stir through the lime juice. Gently stir through the diced avocado and season to taste with salt and pepper.

3. In another bowl, combine the soured cream, mayonnaise and chilli paste until nicely rippled.

4. Stir the rice into the spicy beef mixture and reheat until everything is properly warmed through.

5. Heat the tortillas in a dry frying pan over a medium heat for 1 minute on each side. Lay a tortilla flat in front of you. Spoon a quarter of the beef and rice mixture horizontally across the middle, leaving a gap at either end. Top with the avocado and tomato salad, a drizzle of the soured cream dressing and some of the shredded lettuce and grated cheese (if using). Turn the two ends inwards and tightly roll up the tortilla away from you. Slice into four and wrap each piece in foil, then repeat with the remaining tortillas.

6. Serve on a platter with some chilli sauce for people to shake over.

CHARD, TALEGGIO AND CHORIZO EMPANADAS

Little pastry parcels filled with anything from juicy prawns to spicy beef to these chard and chorizo ones. Empanadas make a great pick-up treat – perfect for sharing around while they are still warm or for wrapping up for a picnic.

MAKES 14 EMPANADAS
PREP: 35 MINUTES, PLUS CHILLING
COOK: 50–55 MINUTES

400g (14oz/3⅓ cups) plain (all-purpose) flour, plus extra for dusting
100g (3½oz/1⅔ cups) coarse cornmeal, plus extra for sprinkling
130g (4½oz/½ cup) cold unsalted butter, cubed
1 medium free-range egg yolk, plus 2 yolks, beaten, to glaze
100ml (3½fl oz/½ cup) ice-cold water
Salt and black pepper
Smoky Chipotle and Tomato Chutney (page 100), to serve (optional)

FOR THE FILLING

150g (5oz) waxy potatoes (such as Désirée), peeled and diced into 1cm (½in) cubes
1 tbsp olive oil
3 banana shallots, peeled and sliced
170g (6oz) cooking chorizo, diced
1 fat garlic clove, crushed
200g (7oz) chard or spinach, chopped
Zest of 1 lemon
Leaves of 1 small bunch of parsley, finely chopped
100g (3½oz) Taleggio, chopped, or grated mozzarella

You may need a 12cm (5in) pastry cutter

1. Place the flour, cornmeal and 1 teaspoon of salt in a food processor and pulse to combine. Add the butter and pulse until the mixture resembles fine breadcrumbs. Whisk the egg yolk with the ice-cold water. Add to the mix and pulse until the mixture comes together. Add a dash more water (up to 50ml) if it seems dry. Knead briefly until it comes together and feels smooth. Wrap in cling film (plastic wrap) and chill for 1 hour.

2. Next prepare the filling. Bring a saucepan of salted water to the boil. Add the diced potato to the pan and parboil for 3–4 minutes. Drain in a colander and steam dry for 5 minutes.

3. Heat the olive oil in a frying pan (skillet) over a medium heat. Add the shallots and a pinch of salt and cook for 7–10 minutes until softened and turning golden. Turn up the heat, add the chorizo and fry for 3–5 minutes or until it is beginning to go brown. Stir through the garlic, cooking for 1 minute. Add the chard or spinach and cook for 4 minutes or until wilted.

4. Remove from the heat and tip into a bowl, then stir through the diced potato, lemon zest and parsley. Season and allow to cool down for 30 minutes before gently mixing in the cheese.

5. Preheat the oven to 180°C (160°C fan)/350°F/gas 4 and line a baking tray (cookie sheet) with baking parchment.

6. Divide the chilled dough in half and roll each out to about 3mm (⅓in) thick, then cut into 12cm (5in) rounds with the pastry cutter or by cutting round the rim of a small bowl.

7. Add a heaped tablespoon of the filling onto the centre of each round, brush the edges with beaten egg yolk and fold over, then seal firmly by crimping the edges with a fork. Brush the top with a little more egg yolk and sprinkle over a little extra cornmeal. Place on the prepared baking tray and bake for 30 minutes or until light golden brown. Serve with a dollop of chipotle chutney.

FIERY HABANERO CHICKEN WINGS

A few spoonfuls of the homemade habanero sauce on page 101 is all you need to fire up these sticky charred chicken wings. In the summer, try barbecuing them and pass around with a pot of the Mexican-style herby crema to cool them down.

MAKES 10–12 CHICKEN WINGS
PREP: 15 MINUTES, PLUS MARINATING
COOK: 35–45 MINUTES

10–12 large chicken wings

4 tbsp Fiery Habanero Chilli Sauce (page 101)

1 heaped tsp sweet smoked paprika

2 fat garlic cloves, finely grated

6 tbsp runny honey

2 tbsp tomato ketchup

2 tbsp Worcestershire sauce

1 tsp salt

½ bunch of spring onions (scallions), sliced on the diagonal

2 medium-sized fresh red chillies, sliced

Lime wedges, to serve

FOR THE CREMA

100g (3½oz/scant ½ cup) soured cream

2 rounded tbsp mayonnaise

Leaves of ½ small bunch of parsley, very finely chopped

Leaves of ½ small bunch of coriander (cilantro), very finely chopped

1. Place the chicken wings in a bowl, add the chilli sauce, paprika, garlic, honey, tomato ketchup, Worcestershire sauce and salt and toss together, making sure the chicken is well coated. Cover the bowl and set aside in the fridge for 24 hours.

2. Preheat the oven to 200°C (180°C fan)/400°F/gas 6.

3. Heat a ridged griddle pan or non-stick frying pan (skillet) over a high heat until almost at smoking point. Add the chicken to the pan in batches and cook on each side for 3–4 minutes until blistered. Transfer the cooked chicken to a baking tray (cookie sheet) or roasting pan and brush over any remaining marinade, then roast in the oven for a further 20–25 minutes or until the chicken is cooked through.

4. In a small bowl, combine the soured cream, mayonnaise, parsley and half the coriander.

5. Spread the charred chicken wings on a serving plate and top with the remaining coriander and the sliced spring onions and chillies. Serve with the crema and wedges of lime to squeeze over the chicken.

CHEESY PULL-APART QUESADILLAS

If you haven't yet invited your friends over for a few cocktails and plates of hot, gooey quesadillas, now is the time. Ditch your takeaway pizzas and slice these up to share with friends, mixing and matching these delicious cheesy fillings.

BLACK BEAN AND FONTINA CHEESE

SERVES 2–4
PREP: 15 MINUTES
COOK: 25 MINUTES

1 tbsp olive oil

1 banana shallot, finely sliced

1 garlic clove, crushed

1 tsp sweet smoked paprika

1 tsp ground coriander

½ x 400g can chopped tomatoes

1 tbsp (light soft) brown sugar

½ x 400g can black beans, drained
   and rinsed

½ large bunch of coriander (cilantro),
   roughly chopped

2 large flour tortillas

80g (3oz) fontina cheese, sliced, or
   grated mozzarella

1 fresh green jalapeño chilli,
   thinly sliced

2 tbsp Pink Pickled Onions (page 104),
   drained

Salt and black pepper

1. Heat the olive oil in a medium frying pan (skillet) over a medium heat, add the shallot, along with a pinch of salt, and fry for 7–10 minutes or until beginning to soften and turn golden brown. Add the garlic and cook for another minute. Stir through the spices and cook for a further 2 minutes.

2. Add the tomatoes and brown sugar to the pan. Bring to a simmer and cook for 10 minutes or until the liquid is reduced by half. Tip the beans into the pan, along with half the coriander, and stir through. Heat through for a few minutes, then season to taste with salt and pepper and remove from the heat.

3. Heat a non-stick frying pan over a medium-high heat until almost at smoking point. Place one of the tortillas in the pan, top with the bean mixture and the cheese and cover with the second tortilla. Use something heavy, such as a saucepan, to place on top of the quesadilla to weight it down. Cook on each side for 1–2 minutes or until golden brown and molten in the centre.

4. Slice the quesadilla into six wedges and serve topped with the sliced chilli, the remaining coriander and a bundle of pickled onions, if you like.

CROQUE-MONSIEUR QUESADILLA

SERVES 2–4
PREP: 15 MINUTES
COOK: 10 MINUTES

25g (1oz/2 tbsp) unsalted butter

1 tbsp plain (all-purpose) flour

120ml (4fl oz/½ cup) whole milk

2 tsp Dijon mustard

A good pinch of freshly grated nutmeg

3 slices of thick smoked ham

70g (2½oz) Comté or mature
   Cheddar, grated

2 large flour tortillas

Salt and black pepper

1 large free-range fried egg, to serve
   (optional),

1. First make the béchamel sauce. Melt the butter in a medium saucepan over a low heat until beginning to foam. Stir through the flour and cook for another minute. Remove from the heat and whisk in the milk, then return to the heat and allow to bubble for a further 2–3 minutes, stirring constantly. Whisk in the mustard and nutmeg and season to taste with salt and pepper.

2. Preheat the grill (broiler) to medium. Line a baking tray (cookie sheet) with foil and lay one of the tortillas on it. Pop under the grill to cook on one side for 2–3 minutes or until just beginning to turn a light golden brown. Top with the smoked ham and two-thirds of the cheese. Place the second tortilla on top and spread over the béchamel sauce with the back of a spoon. Top with the remaining cheese and cook under the grill for 3–4 minutes or until golden and bubbling.

3. Top with a fried egg, if you like, as part of a breakfast spread, then cut into six triangular wedges and pull the gooey quesadilla apart!

MUSHROOM, CHARRED SPRING ONION AND BLUE CHEESE

SERVES 2–4
PREP: 15 MINUTES
COOK: 20 MINUTES

1 tbsp olive oil

6 spring onions (scallions), trimmed

1 tbsp unsalted butter

100g (3½oz) chestnut mushrooms, sliced

100g (3½oz) portobello mushrooms, sliced

1 small garlic clove, crushed

Leaves of 2 sprigs thyme, chopped, plus extra to serve

50g (2oz) blue cheese (such as Saint Agur), crumbled

30g (1oz/⅓ cup) grated mozzarella

2 large flour tortillas

Salt and black pepper

Soured cream, to serve

1. Heat a ridged griddle pan or non-stick frying pan (skillet) over a high heat until almost at smoking point. Drizzle half the olive oil over the spring onions, add them to the pan and cook for 3–4 minutes on each side until softened and charred. Set aside on a plate.

2. Heat the butter and remaining oil together in a medium frying pan over a medium heat until the butter melts and begins to foam. Add all the mushrooms and fry for 7 minutes or until softened and beginning to turn golden brown. Add the garlic and thyme and cook for a further 5 minutes. Season with salt and pepper to taste.

3. Mix together the blue cheese and mozzarella. Heat a large non-stick frying pan over a medium-high heat until almost at smoking point. Place one of the tortillas in the pan, then spread with the mushroom mixture, add the charred spring onions and sprinkle over the cheese. Top with the second tortilla and use something heavy, such as a saucepan, to place on top of the quesadilla to weight it down. Cook for 1–2 minutes before carefully turning over and repeating on the other side.

4. Scatter a little extra fresh thyme over the quesadilla, slice into six triangular wedges and serve with soured cream.

PAN CORNBREAD WITH CHARRED SPRING ONION CREAM CHEESE

Warm wedges of cornbread are smeared with thick spring onion cream cheese in this crowd-pleasing recipe. Cornmeal is sometimes branded as polenta and you can easily find it in the world food section of supermarkets. Avoid the quick-cook polenta, though, as this isn't the same. Once cooked, share these round straight from the oven or serve with the Veggie Chilli on page 52.

SERVES 6–8
PREP: 25 MINUTES, PLUS SOAKING
COOK: 20 MINUTES

150g (5oz/1 scant cup) coarse cornmeal or polenta

250ml (9fl oz/1 cup) buttermilk

70g (2½oz/⅓ cup) salted butter

50g (2oz/½ cup) plain (all-purpose) flour

2 tbsp (light soft) brown sugar

1 tsp chipotle or standard chilli flakes

1 tsp baking powder

½ tsp bicarbonate of soda (baking soda)

2 fresh green jalapeños or 1 fresh red chilli, deseeded and finely chopped

2 medium free-range eggs, lightly beaten

30g (1oz) Parmesan, finely grated

30g (1oz) mature Cheddar, grated

Salt and black pepper

FOR THE SPRING ONION CREAM CHEESE

1 tbsp olive oil

1 bunch of spring onions (scallions), trimmed

1 x 180g tub of cream cheese

2 tbsp soured cream

1. Tip half the cornmeal/polenta into a bowl, pour over the buttermilk and leave to soak for a minimum of 3 hours or overnight in the fridge.

2. Preheat the oven to 220°C (200°C fan)/425°F/gas 7.

3. Melt the butter in a 20cm (8in) deep ovenproof frying pan (skillet), swirling the pan to coat the edges.

4. Tip the remaining cornmeal into the soaked mixture and stir in the flour, sugar, chilli flakes, baking powder, bicarbonate of soda and ½ teaspoon of salt, followed by the chopped chillies, beaten eggs, melted butter and grated cheeses. Pour the mixture into the pan in which you melted the butter and bake in the oven for 15–20 minutes or until golden brown and firm to the touch. Set aside to cool down a little.

5. Meanwhile, heat a ridged griddle pan or non-stick frying pan over a high heat until almost at smoking point. Drizzle the olive oil over the spring onions and add them to the hot pan. Cook for 3–4 minutes on each side or until charred and softened. Transfer to a chopping board and roughly chop. Leave to cool down slightly, then place in the small bowl of a food processor with the cream cheese and soured cream. Whizz until smooth and creamy and season to taste with salt and pepper.

6. Cut the cornbread into thick wedges and serve smeared with the cream cheese.

PINT OF PRAWNS WITH CHOLULA MARIE ROSE

The easiest-ever bar snack. Juicy whole prawns stuffed into a pint glass and served with mayo spiked with Mexican Cholula chilli sauce. Enjoy with some wedges of lime and crack open a few ice-cold beers!

SERVES 2
PREP: 10 MINUTES

400g (14oz) large or small cooked
   prawns (shrimp) with shells

Sourdough bread, to serve (optional)

FOR THE CHOLULA MARIE ROSE SAUCE

100g (3½oz/scant ½ cup) good-quality
   mayonnaise

1 tbsp Cholula or other chilli sauce

2 tsp tomato ketchup

A pinch of sweet smoked paprika

Zest of 1 lime, plus wedges to serve

You may also need 2 x 600ml (1 pint)
glasses

1. Spoon the mayonnaise into a bowl and stir through the chilli sauce, tomato ketchup, paprika and lime zest.

2. Pile the cooked prawns into two large pint glasses or a bowl and serve with the Cholula Marie Rose sauce and wedges of lime. Serve on its own or with some sourdough bread. If you like it hotter, shake a little extra of the chilli sauce onto your peeled prawns!

4

SALSAS
AND PICKLES

VINE-RIPENED TOMATO SALSA

A staple accompaniment for any Mexican meal is a fresh homemade salsa and one made with vine-ripened tomatoes is a great starting point. Heat it up by swapping the green chillies for red, and in the summer use a mixture of colourful heritage tomatoes. Serve it at a barbecue with a giant bowl of salty tortilla chips (pages 42–43) or simply piled on top of a charred ribeye steak on a Friday night.

SERVES 4–6
PREP: 15 MINUTES, PLUS CHILLING

500g (1lb 2oz) vine-ripened tomatoes
  (large or cherry)

¼ small red onion, finely chopped

1 spring onion (scallion), finely sliced

Leaves of 1 small handful of coriander
  (cilantro), shredded

Juice of ½ lime

1 large fresh green or red chilli,
  deseeded and finely chopped

½ small garlic clove, finely grated

½ tsp fine salt

1. Halve the tomatoes and scoop out the seeds with a teaspoon, then finely chop the flesh and transfer to a mortar. Bash the chopped tomatoes for a few minutes using a pestle.

2. Stir through the red onion, spring onion and coriander, followed by the lime juice, chilli, garlic and salt. Cover and chill in the fridge for a minimum of 1 hour, or ideally overnight, to allow the flavours to develop.

PICO DE GALLO SALSA

Unlike tomato salsa (see opposite) this is more of a chopped salad. With a fresh flavour and chunkier texture, each ingredient is distinct in the bowl and it doesn't have the wet sauciness of its sister dish. The chopped coriander and juicy pieces of tomato make it perfect spooned on top of tacos. You can't venture into Mexican cuisine without trying this classic!

SERVES 4–6
PREP: 15 MINUTES

400g (14oz) large vine-ripened
   tomatoes

1 large banana shallot, very finely
   chopped

1 small fresh jalapeño or other mild
   green chilli, deseeded and finely
   chopped

1 small bunch of coriander (cilantro),
   finely chopped

Zest of 1 large lime

½ tsp fine salt

1. Halve the tomatoes and scoop out the seeds with a teaspoon. Finally dice the tomato flesh and transfer to a bowl. Add the shallot and gently combine with the chopped tomatoes.

2. Add the chilli to the bowl with the other chopped ingredients and stir through the coriander, lime zest and salt. Eat immediately or keep for up to 2 days, covered, in the fridge.

GREEN TOMATILLO SALSA

A little smaller and greener than a tomato, a tomatillo is a Mexican fruit that is ideal for blitzing into a juicy salsa. Eaten on its own or mixed with creamy avocado, it's milder and slightly fruitier-tasting than a tomato. Getting hold of fresh tomatillos isn't always easy, but canned ones are readily available online these days and work just as well. You'll find that they come in a very large can; any that you don't use in the salsa are delicious simply chopped and stirred through guacamole (page 102).

SERVES 4–6
PREP: 10 MINUTES

1 small bunch of coriander (cilantro)

1 small garlic clove, sliced

1 mild fresh green chilli, deseeded
   and sliced

¼ small red onion, chopped

270g (10oz/1¼ cups) canned whole
   tomatillos, drained and lightly rinsed

¼ tsp golden caster (superfine) sugar

½ tbsp white wine vinegar

1. Place the whole bunch of coriander in the small bowl of a food processor with the garlic, chilli and onion and pulse until finally chopped. Transfer to a bowl.

2. Add the tomatillos to the food processor, along with the sugar and vinegar, and blitz again until just combined. Tip into the bowl with the coriander and onion mixture and stir together.

3. Transfer to a serving bowl and eat with tortilla chips (pages 42–43), or stir a few spoonfuls of the salsa into creamy mashed avocado and pile on to warm tacos. Eat the salsa immediately or keep for up to 2 days, covered, in the fridge.

BLISTERED-AND-CHARRED-CHILLI SALSA

A real favourite in the salsa world, this medley of charred chillies and vegetables is packed with smoky tones. The veg are best cooked on a griddle pan or barbecue but you could use a smoking-hot frying pan (skillet) instead. The salsa is delicious if left to develop its flavour – it can be stored in the fridge overnight – but it's also great eaten warm from the bowl with soft tortillas (page 16) to scoop it up.

SERVES 4–6
PREP: 10 MINUTES
COOK: 10–15 MINUTES

½ small red onion, quartered

1 large fresh red chilli

1 large fresh green jalapeño chilli

2 fat garlic cloves, peeled

3 medium plum or vine-ripened
   tomatoes, quartered

1 tbsp extra-virgin olive oil, plus extra
   for drizzling

1 tsp red wine vinegar

½ tsp fine salt

1. Heat a ridged griddle pan or non-stick frying pan over a medium-high heat until almost at smoking point. Add the onion, chillies, garlic and tomatoes to the pan and cook, using tongs or two forks to regularly turn the vegetables, for 10–15 minutes or until each one is charred and beginning to soften (the tomatoes will take the least time). Cook in batches, if needed, depending on the size of your pan.

2. Halve and deseed the cooked chillies and roughly chop with the rest of the charred vegetables. Add to a food processor or large mortar, along with the oil and vinegar, and blitz in the processor or bash roughly with a pestle. Season to taste with the salt.

3. Spoon into a serving bowl and drizzle over a little more olive oil, if you like.

SMOKY CHIPOTLE AND TOMATO CHUTNEY

Chutney might sound daunting and time-consuming to make, but it's actually super-simple. The trick is to let it bubble and reduce for long enough on the hob. All you need is a punnet of supermarket tomatoes and a generous spoonful of good-quality chipotle paste to make this smoky number. Keep it in the fridge to pep up a fried egg on toast, or serve after dinner on a cheese board with crumbly mature Cheddar or another hard cheese like Lincolnshire Poacher, if you're feeling fancy!

MAKES 1 X 500ML (18FL OZ) JAR
PREP: 10 MINUTES
COOK: 1¼ – 1½ HOURS

1kg (2lb 3oz) plum tomatoes, halved

2 tbsp olive oil

4 whole garlic cloves

2 tbsp chipotle chilli paste

½ tsp hot smoked paprika

4 tbsp balsamic vinegar

3 tbsp (soft light) brown sugar

1 small bunch of oregano,
   roughly chopped

Salt and black pepper

You will also need a 500ml (18fl oz) sterilised jar with a lid. To sterilise it, first wash thoroughly in hot, soapy water, then place the jar upside down on a wire rack in the oven, preheated to 140°C (120°C fan)/275°F/gas 1, with the lid next to it, and heat through for 15 minutes. Remove and use as soon as possible.

1. Preheat the oven to 200°C (180°C fan)/400°F/gas 6.

2. Arrange the halved tomatoes, cut side down, on a large baking tray (cookie sheet). Drizzle over the olive oil, nestle the garlic among the tomato halves and season generously with salt and pepper. Place in the oven to roast for 25–30 minutes or until the tomatoes are broken down and softened.

3. Tip the roasted tomatoes into a large saucepan. Pop the garlic flesh out of the skins, roughly chop and add to the tomato mixture, along with the chipotle paste and paprika. Stir through the vinegar and sugar.

4. Bring to the boil, then reduce the heat and simmer, uncovered, for 50–60 minutes until reduced and thickened. Season to taste with salt and pepper and stir through the fresh oregano.

5. Spoon into the sterilised jar and allow to cool down for 15 minutes before sealing the jar tightly with the lid. Store in the fridge for up to 4 weeks and keep for up to 2 weeks once opened.

FIERY HABANERO CHILLI SAUCE

Not for the faint-hearted. If you like it hot, this is the sauce for you. A mere dab will blow your head off. Use with caution to stir through a sauce or toss with the chicken wings on page 82. Either way, it's a scorcher!

MAKES 1 X 200ML (7FL OZ) JAR
PREP: 10 MINUTES
COOK: 5 MINUTES

2 dried red habanero chillies

4 ripe plum tomatoes

1 tbsp cider vinegar

2 tbsp tomato purée

1½ tbsp (soft light) brown sugar

1 fat garlic clove, peeled

Salt

You will also need a 200ml (7fl oz) sterilised jar with a lid. To sterilise it, first wash thoroughly in hot, soapy water, then place the jar upside down on a wire rack in the oven, preheated to 140°C (120°C fan)/275°F/gas 1, with the lid next to it, and heat through for 15 minutes. Remove and use as soon as possible.

1. Place the dried chillies in a small pan of water and bring to the boil. Lower the heat to a simmer and cook for 5 minutes. Drain and then carefully remove the stalks and seeds from the chillies and discard.

2. Cut a small slit in the base of each plum tomato. Leave the tomatoes in a bowl of boiling water for 3 minutes, then gently peel away the skin, deseed and roughly chop the flesh.

3. Tip the chillies into a blender or the small bowl of a food processor, along with the chopped tomatoes, vinegar, tomato purée, sugar and garlic. Blitz until smooth and season to taste with salt.

4. Spoon into the sterilised jar and seal the jar tightly with the lid. Store in the fridge for up to 2 weeks and keep for up to 5 days once opened.

GUACAMOLE

Avocados seem to have crept into everyone's supermarket trolley in the last few years, and who can blame us! They're pretty special, it has to be said. These green-fleshed, creamy fruits are great smashed and spread on a slice of sourdough, and even better with a few extra ingredients folded through. Try this ultimate guacamole. Up the chilli if you like it spicy, but don't use less than ½ teaspoon of salt – it makes all the difference.

SERVES 4–6
PREP: 10 MINUTES

2 large ripe avocados

¼ small red onion, very finely chopped

1 small fresh red chilli, deseeded and finely chopped

1 small garlic clove, finely grated

½ small bunch of coriander (cilantro), very finely chopped

Juice of 1–2 limes (to taste)

½ tsp fine salt

Avocado oil or extra-virgin olive oil, for drizzling (optional)

1. Halve and carefully remove the stone from each avocado. Use a spoon to scoop the flesh from the skins and into a bowl. Gently mash the avocado with a fork, taking care to keep some nice chunky nuggets of the green flesh.

2. Stir through the onion, chilli, garlic, coriander and lime juice. Season with the salt and serve immediately, drizzled with oil if you like, or keep in the fridge for up to 2 days with one of the avocado stones nestled in the guacamole to prevent it from going brown.

PINK PICKLED ONIONS

Every taco is in need of a basic topping and a bundle of these bright pink pickles should fit the bill nicely. They cut through rich meats and oily fish and will soon become a staple if you're an avid Mexican food fan. Give them a go – super-easy and mega-moreish. You can eat the pickled onions as soon as they've cooled down. If not storing them in a jar, they can be kept in a bowl in the fridge for up to 5 days.

MAKES I X 500ML (18FL OZ) JAR
PREP: 15 MINUTES
COOK: 5 MINUTES

200ml (7fl oz/¾ cup) white
   wine vinegar

100ml (3½fl oz/½ cup) water

4 tbsp caster (superfine) sugar

1 tbsp salt

1 tbsp coriander seeds

1 tsp black peppercorns

½ tsp chilli flakes

2 bay leaves

2 medium or 3 small red onions, halved
   and finely sliced

You will also need a 500ml (18fl oz) sterilised jar with a lid. To sterilise it, first wash thoroughly in hot, soapy water, then place the jar upside down on a wire rack in the oven, preheated to 140°C (120°C fan)/275°F/gas 1, with the lid next to it, and heat through for 15 minutes. Remove and use as soon as possible.

1. Pour the vinegar and water into a medium saucepan. Add the sugar, salt, coriander seeds, peppercorns, chilli flakes and bay leaves and bring to the boil. Reduce the heat and simmer for 5 minutes or until the sugar has dissolved. Remove from the heat and pour into a jug.

2. Place the sliced onions in a large bowl and cover with boiling water. Set aside for 5–10 minutes or until the onions have begun to soften. Drain and pack into the sterilised jar. Pour over the pickling liquid.

3. Seal tightly with the lid and store in the fridge for up to 3 weeks, keeping for up to 1 week once opened. Although they will gradually lose their vibrant pink colour the longer you leave them, the pickles will still taste delicious.

EASY PICKLED JALAPEÑOS

A big jar of homemade pickled jalapeños is so handy to have stored on a shelf or sitting in your fridge. Crack open a jar and pile on top of nachos with soured cream and salsa, or throw them into a sandwich stuffed with cheese and fry in butter for an epic, gooey chilli-cheese toasty.

MAKES I X I LITRE (1¾ PINT) JAR
PREP: 15 MINUTES, PLUS COOLING
COOK: 5 MINUTES

250ml (9fl oz/1 cup) white
    wine vinegar

250ml (9fl oz/1 cup) water

6 tbsp caster (superfine) sugar

1 tbsp salt

1 tbsp coriander seeds

450g (1lb) fresh green jalapeño chillies,
    sliced into 1cm (½in) rounds

2 fat garlic cloves, peeled

You will also need a 1 litre (1¾ pint) sterilised jar with a lid. To sterilise it, first wash thoroughly in hot, soapy water, then place the jar upside down on a wire rack in the oven, preheated to 140°C (120°C fan)/275°F/gas 1, with the lid next to it, and heat through for 15 minutes. Remove and use as soon as possible.

1. Pour the vinegar and water into a medium saucepan and add the sugar, salt and coriander seeds. Bring to the boil, then reduce the heat and simmer for 5 minutes, stirring occasionally with a wooden spoon, until the sugar has completely dissolved. Remove from the heat and pour into a jug.

2. Bundle the sliced jalapeños into the sterilised jar and add the garlic cloves. Pour over the pickling liquid and allow to cool down for 15 minutes before sealing the jar tightly with the lid. Store for up to 6 weeks and, once opened, keep in the fridge for up to 2 weeks.

ZESTY LIME AIOLI

A few Mexican twists have been added to this French dip. Whizzing up your own aioli is easy once you get the hang of it. Try not to be too hasty with the oil; slowly drizzling it in helps to amalgamate the mixture and prevent it from splitting. This, or any of the variations included below, would be delicious smeared on top of tacos.

SERVES 6–8
PREP: 15 MINUTES

3 medium free-range egg yolks

150ml (5fl oz/⅔ cup) extra-virgin olive oil

150ml (5fl oz/⅔ cup) sunflower oil

2–3 large limes: juice of 2–3 and zest of 2

½ rounded tsp Dijon mustard

1 small garlic clove, finely grated
or crushed

Salt and black pepper

1. Place the egg yolks in the small bowl of a food processor, along with a pinch of salt. Mix together the two oils and very slowly trickle them into the processor via the feeder tube as the machine is mixing the yolks. Once you've used two-thirds of the oil, you can pour in the rest more quickly. If the mayonnaise beings to split, add a splash of the lime juice.

2. Stir through the remaining lime juice, along with the lime zest, mustard and garlic. If the mayonnaise looks a little thick, add a tablespoon or two of cold water to loosen. You should have a nice glossy aioli.

3. Season well with salt and pepper, then cover and keep in a small bowl in the fridge for up to 3 days.

VARIATIONS

CHIPOTLE AIOLI: Make as above and swirl in 3 teaspoons of shop-bought chipotle chilli paste at the end.

PICKLED JALAPEÑO AIOLI: Make as above, replacing the limes with 2 tablespoons of cider vinegar. Add 60g (2oz/⅔ cup) Easy Pickled Jalapeños (see opposite), drained and deseeded; 1 small fresh green jalapeño, deseeded and sliced; and a handful of fresh coriander (cilantro). No need to add any water to this one; it should be loose enough.

ROASTED GARLIC AIOLI: Preheat the oven to 200°C (180°C fan)/400°F/gas 6. Take a small whole garlic bulb, drizzle with a little olive oil, wrap tightly in foil and place on a baking tray (cookie sheet). Roast in the oven for 45 minutes until the cloves are soft, then allow to cool before squeezing the flesh from the cloves. Make the aioli as above, replacing the limes with 2 lemons and the raw garlic with the roasted garlic flesh whizzed in at the end.

EASY-PEASY AIOLI: Mix some good-quality shop-bought mayonnaise with any of the above flavourings for a super-easy instant aioli.

5

SWEET
THINGS

CHURROS

These curly, deep-fried doughnut-like treats are a Mexican street-food staple. While hot, they are rolled in cinnamon-spiked sugar. You can serve them with a pot of salted caramel or chocolate sauce ... but preferably both.

SERVES 6–8
PREP: 35 MINUTES, PLUS CHILLING
COOK: 25 MINUTES

80g (3oz/⅓ cup) salted butter, melted

300ml (10fl oz/1¼ cups) just-boiled water

1 tsp vanilla extract or vanilla bean paste

300g (11oz/2½ cups) plain (all-purpose) flour

1 large free-range egg yolk

70g (3oz/⅓ cup) golden caster (superfine) sugar

1 heaped tsp ground cinnamon

2 litres (3½ pints/8 cups) sunflower oil

Fine salt

FOR THE SALTED CARAMEL SAUCE

130g (4½oz/⅔ cup) sugar

6 tbsp water

20g (¾oz/1¾ tbsp) unsalted butter

6 tbsp double (heavy) cream

¼ tsp vanilla extract

½ tsp sea salt flakes

FOR THE CHOCOLATE SAUCE

100g (3½oz) dark chocolate (min. 70 per cent cocoa solids), broken into bits

25ml (1fl oz/⅛ cup) double (heavy) cream

25ml (1fl oz/⅛ cup) whole milk

1 tbsp golden (corn) syrup

1 tbsp spiced rum or amaretto

You will also need a disposable piping bag and a 1cm (½in) star nozzle

1. To make the batter, pour the melted butter and just-boiled water into a jug, add the vanilla and mix together. Sift the flour into a large bowl with ¼ teaspoon salt and make a well in the centre. Pour the wet ingredients into the flour and use a wooden spoon to vigorously mix together until you have smooth batter that is pulling away from the bowl. Quickly beat in the egg yolk until fully incorporated. If the mixture is a little dry add up to 50ml of extra water.

2. Slip the nozzle inside the piping bag and put the bag, with the nozzle facing down, into a clean jug to make it easier to fill. Spoon generous dollops of the batter into the piping bag and set aside in the fridge for 30 minutes.

3. Make the salted caramel sauce. Place the sugar and water in a saucepan over a medium heat. Once the sugar has dissolved, raise the heat and gently boil. Do not stir at any stage, but swirl the pan lightly. Once the caramel is golden brown, remove from the heat and swirl in the butter. Quickly beat in the cream and add the vanilla extract and sea salt flakes – be careful as the caramel will be extremely hot. Set aside and gently warm up just before serving.

4. Next make the chocolate sauce. Fill a small saucepan with 2cm (just under 1in) of water and bring to a simmer. Place the chocolate in a heatproof bowl large enough to sit on top of the pan, making sure the base of the bowl doesn't touch the water. Melt the chocolate gently and then whisk in the cream, milk, golden syrup and rum or amaretto. Stir in a pinch of salt and keep warm over a very low heat.

5. Line a baking tray (cookie sheet) with kitchen paper (paper towels). Combine the caster sugar and cinnamon

CONTINUES ON THE NEXT PAGE

and sprinkle over a second tray. Heat the oil in a deep-fryer, or in a large, deep heavy-based saucepan filled no more than two-thirds full, until the oil reaches 160–180°C (325–350°F) on a cooking thermometer. Alternatively, drop in a small cube of bread; it should turn golden brown within 30 seconds.

6. Snip the end off your piping bag and pipe three churros into the hot oil, each 8–10 cm (3–4in) long, snipping them with a pair of scissors. Fry the churros in batches of three, cooking each batch for 5–6 minutes or until golden brown. Remove from the hot oil with a slotted spoon and place on the lined baking tray. Keep warm in a low oven while you make the rest of the churros before liberally coating them in the cinnamon sugar.

7. Serve the churros hot on a large plate with separate bowls of the two dipping sauces to dunk into.

CHURROS ICE-CREAM SANDWICHES

Swirl the churros batter into thick spiralled disks then sandwich them with balls of ice cream for an indulgent treat!

SERVES 4
PREP: 30 MINUTES, PLUS CHILLING
COOK: 30 MINUTES

80g (3oz/⅓ cup) salted butter, melted

300ml (10fl oz/1¼ cups) just-boiled water

1 tsp vanilla extract or vanilla bean paste

300g (11oz/2½ cups) plain (all-purpose) flour

1 large free-range egg yolk

70g (3oz/⅓ cup) golden caster (superfine) sugar

1 heaped tsp ground cinnamon

2 litres (3½ pints/8 cups) sunflower oil

1. Follow the batter recipe according to the method in the recipe on page 110.

2. Cut out eight 8cm (3in) squares baking parchment and place them on a flat baking tray (cookie sheet). Snip the end off your piping bag, to expose the nozzle, then pipe a swirl onto each square. Start in the middle and work outwards in a spiral until you have a round shape about 7cm (3in) in diameter. Place the tray in the fridge for 30 minutes.

3. Line a baking tray with kitchen paper (paper towels). Combine the caster sugar and cinnamon and sprinkle over a second tray. Heat the oil in a deep-fryer, or in a large, deep heavy-based saucepan filled no more than two-thirds full, until the oil reaches 160–180°C (325–350°F) on a cooking thermometer. Alternatively, drop in a small cube of bread; it should turn golden brown within 30 seconds.

Fine salt

Cinnamon (see below), chocolate or
salted-caramel ice cream, to serve

Chocolate Sauce (page 110), to serve
(optional)

*You will also need a disposable piping bag
and a 1cm (½in) star nozzle*

4. Once hot, carefully lower each churro on its piece of paper into the oil and fry for 6–7 minutes, two at a time. Remove the paper from the hot oil with a pair of tongs and discard. Once each churro is golden brown, place on the lined baking tray and keep warm in a low oven.

5. Toss the warm churros in the cinnamon sugar until evenly coated. Scoop a generous ball of ice cream and sandwich between two of the churros, then drizzle over a little chocolate sauce, if you like.

CINNAMON ICE CREAM

Making an ice cream can take a bit of effort, but it's well worth it for the delicious end result – especially this one with its hint of warming spice to offset the creaminess. Spoon into bowls at a party or sandwich between the Churros Ice-Cream Sandwiches (see opposite) for an indulgent treat!

SERVES 8
**PREP: 20 MINUTES, PLUS CHURNING
THE ICE CREAM AND FREEZING**
COOK: 10 MINUTES

400ml (14fl oz/1⅔ cups) whole milk

500ml (18fl oz/2¼ cups) double
(heavy) cream

4 tbsp dark spiced rum

8 medium free-range egg yolks

150g (5oz/¾ cup) golden caster
(superfine) sugar

1 tbsp ground cinnamon

¼ tsp fine salt

You will also need an ice-cream maker

1. Place the milk and cream in a small pan over a medium heat and warm through until the mixture begins to steam; don't let it boil. Remove from the heat and whisk in the rum.

2. In a bowl, whisk together the egg yolks, sugar, cinnamon and salt until pale and creamy. Gradually pour the cream mixture into the egg yolk mixture, whisking continuously.

3. Clean the pan and pour the custard mixture back into it. Warm through over a low heat for 3–4 minutes, stirring continuously with a wooden spoon, until the custard is the consistency of double cream and thick enough to coat the back of the spoon. Don't allow it to boil.

4. Strain the custard through a sieve, to remove any lumps, and allow to cool completely. Churn the mixture in an ice-cream maker for 1 hour, or according to the manufacturer's instructions, then transfer to a freezerproof container with a lid. Cover and freeze for 24 hours. Remove from the freezer 15 minutes before serving.

TRES LECHES CAKE

No Mexican birthday is complete without a hefty wedge of sweet, sticky tres leches cake. The light sponge is soaked in condensed and evaporated milk and then topped with sweet whipped cream – the 'three milks' of its name. This version is finished with desiccated coconut and maraschino cherries – ultra-kitsch and flippin' delicious!

SERVES 12
PREP: 25 MINUTES, PLUS CHILLING
COOK: 30–35 MINUTES

5 large free-range eggs

¼ tsp fine salt

225g (8oz/1 cup) caster (superfine) sugar

120g (4½oz/½ cup) unsalted butter, melted, plus extra for greasing

250g (9oz/2 cups) self-raising flour

1½ tsp baking powder

1 tsp vanilla bean paste

6 tbsp whole milk

1 x 397g can condensed milk

1 x 400g can evaporated milk

300ml (10fl oz/1⅔ cups) double (heavy) cream

4 tbsp white coconut rum (such as Malibu)

50g (2oz/generous ½ cup) icing (confectioners') sugar, sifted

40g (1½oz/scant ½ cup) desiccated coconut

1 handful of maraschino cherries, drained, to serve

You will also need a 23 x 23cm (9 x 9in) deep cake tin (pan)

1. Preheat the oven to 180°C (160°C fan)/350°F/gas 4, then grease the sides of the cake tin with butter and line the base with baking parchment.

2. Separate the eggs, placing the whites into a large spotlessly clean bowl and the yolks in another. Whisk the egg whites with an electric whisk into soft fluffy peaks, then add the salt and 50g (2oz/¼ cup) of the caster sugar 1 teaspoon at a time and whisk again until the mixture is stiff and glossy.

3. In the other bowl, whisk together the egg yolks with the remaining sugar and the melted butter until pale and fluffy. Mix in the flour, baking powder, vanilla bean paste and milk. Spoon a third of the whisked egg whites into the yolk mixture to loosen, then very gently fold in the remaining whites, being careful not to knock out too much air.

4. Tip carefully into the prepared tin and bake in the oven for 30–35 minutes until golden brown and firm to the touch. Leave to cool down completely in the tin.

5. In a saucepan over a medium heat, warm through the condensed and evaporated milks until still just cool enough to dip your finger into. Prick holes all over the surface of the sponge with a cocktail stick and gently pour the mix over. Cover with cling film (plastic wrap) and set aside in the fridge for a minimum of 3 hours or overnight.

6. Whisk together the cream, coconut rum and icing sugar until lightly whipped but still creamy. (Try not to over-whip the cream at this stage.) Remove the cake from the fridge and spread over a thick layer of the cream. Finish with a layer of the desiccated coconut and return to the fridge for a final hour before topping with maraschino cherries.

DARK CHOCOLATE, RYE AND CHILLI COOKIES

These molten, dark chocolate cookies are something special. The rye flour gives them a dense texture and rich malty flavour, while a hit of chilli pepper and salt at the end just takes the edge off the chocolate, stopping it from being too rich. To store the cookies and have them ready to bake at any time, simply freeze the raw balls of dough, then bring to room temperature for 20 minutes before baking.

MAKES 15 COOKIES
PREP: 30 MINUTES, PLUS CHILLING
COOK: 10 MINUTES

175g (6oz/generous ⅔ cup) salted butter, softened

200g (7oz/scant 1 cup) (dark soft) brown sugar

80g (3oz/generous ⅓ cup) golden caster (superfine) sugar

1 large free-range egg and 1 large egg yolk

100g (3½oz/generous ¾ cup) plain (all-purpose) flour

120g (4½oz/1 cup) wholemeal (whole wheat) rye flour

40g (1½oz/½ cup) good-quality cocoa powder

½ tsp baking powder

¼ tsp bicarbonate of soda (baking soda)

200g (7oz) dark chocolate (minimum 70 per cent cocoa solids), chopped into rough chunks

1 tsp chilli flakes

Sea salt

1. Place the butter, both sugars and ½ teaspoon of salt into a free-standing electric mixer with a paddle attachment. Beat together the sugar and butter for 10 minutes or until light and fluffy. Alternatively, beat by hand with a wooden spoon for 15 minutes. Whisk the whole egg and extra yolk lightly together in a small bowl. Gradually add to the butter mixture, beating until fully incorporated.

2. Sift both flours into a large bowl with the cocoa powder, baking powder and bicarbonate of soda, making sure to add any of the bran remaining in the sieve. Add the dry ingredients to the butter mixture, along with the chocolate chunks, and turn the mixer on, beating gently, until everything is incorporated. Alternatively, beat together with a wooden spoon. The mixture should be thick and stiff.

3. Divide the mixture into 15 equal-sized pieces. Roll into balls and set aside on a tray lined with non-stick parchment paper. Place in the freezer to chill for 20 minutes.

4. Preheat the oven to 200°C (180°C fan)/400°F/gas 6. Divide the chocolate balls between 2–3 large baking trays (cookie sheets) lined with non-stick baking parchment, being careful to space them so they have enough room to expand as they cook. Sprinkle with the chilli flakes and a little more salt.

5. Bake in the oven for 8–10 minutes, then allow to cool for 10 minutes before transferring to a wire rack. The cookies will firm up as they cool, so don't worry if they seem a little soft at first. Enjoy them warm, and store any remaining cookies in an airtight container for up to 3 days.

HIBISCUS RIPPLE ICE LOLLIES

These fruity ice lollies (popsicles) are made with hibiscus flowers and creamy raspberry ice cream – a truly delicious frozen treat! Popular in Mexico, hibiscus has a tart, berry-rich floral flavour and works beautifully with the creamy contrast of vanilla ice cream in this recipe. Dried hibiscus flowers are available to buy online and in wholefood shops. Traditional lolly moulds are easy to source online as well.

MAKES 10 ICE LOLLIES (POPSICLES)
PREP: 20 MINUTES, PLUS CHILLING
**   AND FREEZING**

25g (1oz/generous ½ cup) edible dried
    hibiscus flowers
130g (4½oz/⅔ cup) caster (superfine)
    sugar
450ml (15fl oz/1¾ cups) boiling water
500ml (18fl oz) vanilla ice cream
100g (3½ oz/1 cup) frozen raspberries

You will also need a 10-hole ice-lolly
    mould and 10 wooden lolly sticks

1. Place the hibiscus flowers and sugar in a bowl and pour over the boiling water. Stir to dissolve the sugar, and leave the hibiscus to infuse in the water until completely cooled, then strain through a sieve set over a jug.

2. Spoon the vanilla ice cream into a large bowl and crumble in the frozen raspberries, pressing down with the back of the spoon to crush them.

3. Pour enough of the strained hibiscus liquid into each section of the lolly mould to fill it halfway, then top with a spoonful or two of ice cream, leaving a small gap at the top of each mould. Tap the ice lolly mould on a kitchen worktop to gently remove any air bubbles. Push in the lolly sticks and freeze overnight.

BROWN SUGAR-ROASTED PINEAPPLE MINI CHEESECAKES

Baking a whole cheesecake can be quite daunting, but these little coconut and pineapple numbers are easy to whip up and are as cute as a button. Pass around to friends at a party or enjoy as an after-dinner treat!

MAKES 12 CHEESECAKES
PREP: 30 MINUTES, PLUS CHILLING
COOK: 50–55 MINUTES

170g (6oz) digestive biscuits
  (Graham crackers)

80g (3oz/⅓ cup) salted butter, melted

700g (1½lb/generous 3 cups) cream
  cheese

1 tsp vanilla bean paste

Zest of 2 large limes, plus extra to serve

100g (3½oz/½ cup) caster sugar

2 medium free-range eggs and
  1 egg yolk

2 tbsp plain (all-purpose) flour

50g (2oz/1 cup) coconut flakes

300g (11oz) pineapple flesh, cut into
  2cm (¾in) chunks

60g (2oz/¼ cup) (light soft)
  brown sugar

20g (¾oz/1¾ tbsp) unsalted butter

*You will also need a 12-hole muffin tray
  and 12 paper cases*

1. Place the biscuits in a large plastic sandwich bag and tightly seal. Crush the biscuits to a fine crumb using a rolling pin. Tip into a bowl and combine with the melted butter.

2. Line the muffin tray with the paper cases and divide the biscuit mixture among them. Press the mixture down firmly using the back of a spoon and chill in the fridge for 30 minutes.

3. Place the cream cheese, vanilla bean paste and lime zest into a large bowl with the caster sugar, eggs (whole eggs and yolk) and flour. Using an electric whisk, beat everything together until smooth and creamy. Pour into a jug.

4. Preheat the oven to 160°C (140°C fan)/325°F/gas 3. Divide the cream cheese mixture among the chilled muffin cases. Bake in the oven for 25–30 minutes or until just set with a slight wobble. Allow to cool for 1 hour before placing in the fridge to cool down completely.

5. Shortly before the cheesecakes have finished cooking, spread the coconut flakes out on a baking tray (cookie sheet) and toast in the oven for about 5 minutes, stirring halfway, until lightly browned. Alternatively, toast in a small pan over a low heat for 3–4 minutes.

6. Once the cheesecakes and coconut flakes have been removed, increase the oven temperature to 200°C (180°C fan)/400°F/gas 6. Spread the pineapple chunks on a non-stick baking tray and toss with the brown sugar, dot over nuggets of the butter and roast for 25 minutes. Leave to cool.

7. Remove the cheesecakes from the fridge and top each with a spoonful of roasted pineapple and a scattering of the toasted coconut flakes as well as some extra pared lime zest.

CHARRED FRUIT WITH POMEGRANATE AND VANILLA MASCARPONE

This bright, tropical fruity platter comprises charred wedges of pineapple and apricot with a sweet vanilla mascarpone to dip them into. Serve as a casual dessert after dinner for your friends to dip into or as part of a fiesta table.

SERVES 6–8
PREP: 20 MINUTES, PLUS COOLING
COOK: 20 MINUTES

130g (4½oz/scant ⅔ cup) mascarpone

3 tbsp thick natural Greek yoghurt

2 tbsp maple syrup

1 tsp vanilla bean paste or vanilla extract

1 large ripe pineapple

4 large apricots or peaches, stoned (pitted) and quartered

3 limes

100g (3½oz/⅔ cup) pomegranate seeds

1. Place the mascarpone and yoghurt in a bowl with 1 tablespoon of the maple syrup and the vanilla bean paste/extract. Beat with a wooden spoon until smooth and creamy and spoon into a serving bowl.

2. Cut the skin off the pineapple using a sharp knife. Slice the flesh into 2cm (¾in) rounds and cut each round into 3–4 strips. Heat a ridged griddle pan or non-stick frying pan (skillet) over a high heat until almost at smoking point. Add the sliced pineapple and quartered apricots or peaches and char on each side for 3–4 minutes; this may need to be done in several batches depending on the size of your pan. Leave to cool down for 15–20 minutes.

3. Make a sweet dressing by whisking together the juice and zest of two of the limes and the remaining maple syrup.

4. Spread the charred fruit on a platter, drizzle over the dressing, scatter over the pomegranate seeds and serve with the vanilla mascarpone scattered with pieces of zest pared from the remaining lime.

6

DRINKS

FOUR MARGARITAS

Four variations, including the classic version and a few cocktail twists! No fiesta is complete without Mexico's most famous tipple!

CLASSIC MARGARITA

SERVES 4
PREP: 10 MINUTES

200ml (7fl oz/¾ cup) tequila

100ml (3½fl oz/½ cup) Cointreau or triple sec

Juice of 2 large limes (squeezed lime halves reserved), plus twists of lime peel to serve

3 tbsp agave syrup or runny honey

2 tbsp fine sea salt

Crushed ice, to serve

You will also need 4 margarita or other small glasses

1. Place the tequila, Cointreau or triple sec, lime juice and agave syrup in a jug or large cocktail shaker and stir or shake everything together well.

2. Scatter the salt over a shallow plate. Rub the rims of the glasses with the squeezed lime halves and dip into the salt to coat. Fill the glasses with crushed ice and pour the margarita mix through a small strainer over the ice. Top each glass with a twist of lime peel.

SUMMER APRICOT AND MINT

This version of a margarita uses delicious apricot nectar and bashed fresh mint. Good-quality apricot juice makes all the difference in this one and is worth tracking down. It's fruitier than its classic sister; perfect on a hot summer's night.

SERVES 4
PREP: 10 MINUTES

200ml (7fl oz/¾ cup) white tequila

Juice of 1 lime (squeezed lime halves reserved)

1 x 410g can apricots in syrup, syrup strained and reserved

Leaves of ½ small bunch of mint, plus extra to serve

1 tbsp caster (superfine) sugar

1 tbsp fine salt

400–500ml (14–18fl oz/1⅔–2 cups) good-quality apricot juice

1–2 fresh apricots, stoned (pitted) and quartered

Crushed ice, to serve

You will also need 4 margarita or other small glasses

1. Pour the tequila, lime juice and reserved apricot syrup into a jug or large cocktail shaker and add half the mint leaves. Stir or shake everything together until well combined.

2. Finely chop the remaining mint leaves and toss with the sugar and salt. Scatter the salt mix over a small plate, then rub the rims of the glasses with the squeezed lime halves and dip the rims into the salt mix. Top each glass with crushed ice, strain over the margarita mix and divide the apricot juice, extra mint and apricot wedges among the glasses. Finish with a segment of tinned apricot on the rim.

RHUBARB AND VANILLA

Forced rhubarb is one of winter's most exciting and vibrant fruits. Making it into a syrup and drinking it in cocktails is the perfect way to enjoy it all year round. Double up on the quantity of syrup, if you like, and keep it in a sterilised jar or bottle until needed. Any leftover rhubarb pulp can be swirled through thick yoghurt and dolloped onto your morning granola.

SERVES 6
PREP: 25 MINUTES, PLUS COOLING
COOK: 10–15 MINUTES

300g (11oz) forced rhubarb stalks, cut into 3cm (1¼in) pieces

130g (4½oz/⅔ cup) caster (superfine) sugar

2 large oranges: juice of 2 and pared zest of 1

150ml (5fl oz/⅔ cup) water

1 tsp vanilla bean paste

Juice of 1 lime (squeezed lime halves reserved)

½ tbsp fine salt

250ml (9fl oz/1 cup) tequila

400–500ml (14–18fl oz/1⅔–2 cups) soda water

Ice cubes, to serve

You will also need 6 margarita or other small glasses

1. Place the rhubarb and all but 1 tablespoon of the sugar in a medium saucepan. Add a strip of orange zest to the pan, along with the juice of the oranges, the water and vanilla bean paste. Cook over a medium heat for 10–15 minutes or until the rhubarb begins to soften and break down. Remove from the heat and leave to sit for 15 minutes.

2. Strain the cooled rhubarb juice through a sieve set over a clean pan and reserve the pulp to use later. Bring the liquid to a simmer and allow to reduce by a third. Remove from the heat and leave to cool down completely.

3. Rub the rim of the glasses with the squeezed lime halves. Mix the remaining sugar with the salt on a small plate and dip the rim of each glass into the sugar mixture.

4. Pour the rhubarb syrup into a jug or large cocktail shaker and add the lime juice, tequila and ice cubes. Whisk everything together in the jug, or shake in the cocktail shaker for about 1 minute, then strain into the glasses and top up with the soda water. Finish by garnishing each glass with a twist of orange zest.

FROZEN WATERMELON AND STRAWBERRY

Warm beers or heavy glasses of red wine have no place on a hot summer's evening, instead try this fruity and refreshing take on a margarita using a fresh fruit purée and pink peppercorns. While fresh strawberries are best in this recipe, frozen ones would also work. If you're short on time, just whizz up all the ingredients until slushy and frothy and pour into glasses without the salt and sugar rim.

SERVES 6
PREP: 20 MINUTES

500g (1lb 2oz) ice cubes

250g (9oz) strawberries

250g (9oz) watermelon flesh, cubed and deseeded

Zest and juice of 2 limes (squeezed lime halves reserved), plus extra zest to serve

3 tbsp agave syrup or icing (confectioners') sugar

250ml (9fl oz/1 cup) tequila

400–500ml (14–18fl oz/1⅔–2 cups) soda water

1 tbsp fine sea salt

2 tbsp caster (superfine) sugar

1 tsp pink peppercorns, crushed

You will also need 6 small tumblers

1. Tip the ice into a food processor and whizz until you have a fine, slushy texture. Transfer to a freezerproof container and store in the freezer until ready to use.

2. Pop the strawberries and watermelon into the food processor, along with lime zest and juice and agave syrup or icing sugar, and blitz until you have a smooth purée. Transfer to a jug and stir through the tequila and soda water.

3. In a shallow dish, mix together the salt, caster sugar and crushed peppercorns. Rub the rims of the tumblers with the squeezed lime halves, then dip each glass into the salt mixture. Pile the crushed ice into the glasses and pour over the fruity mixture. Add a little extra grated lime zest to each glass to finish.

MEXICANA BLOODY MARY

A Mexicana spiced-up version of the savoury cocktail classic. The Tabasco has been swapped for Cholula chilli sauce, while a pinch of smoky chipotle chilli flakes have been added for a hefty punch of heat. Serve alongside the Breakfast Tacos on page 18 for a weekend treat.

SERVES 4
PREP: 10 MINUTES

200ml (7fl oz/¾ cup) vodka

Juice of 1 lime

1 litre (1¾ pints/4¼ cups) good-quality tomato juice

4 tsp Cholula or other chilli sauce

4 tsp Worcestershire sauce

3 tsp celery salt

1 tsp freshly ground black pepper

1 tsp chipotle or standard chilli flakes

4 celery sticks (optional)

Crushed ice, to serve

You will also need 4 tall glasses

1. In a large jug, combine the vodka, lime juice, tomato juice, chilli sauce, Worcestershire sauce and celery salt. Mix everything together well.

2. Fill the glasses a third full with crushed ice, then pour over the Bloody Mary mixture and top with a pinch each of black pepper and chipotle chilli flakes. Add a stick of celery to finish, if you fancy!

THREE AGUAS FRESCAS

Hugely popular in Mexico, aguas frescas, or 'fresh waters', are a wonderfully refreshing non-alcholic drink. They are made by whizzing fruit, edible flowers or even vegetables with ice, cold water and citrus juice. Perfect in the hot summer months!

AGUA DE JAMAICA (HIBISCUS AGUA FRESCA)

A glass of ruby agua de Jamaica, or hibiscus iced tea, is super-easy to whip up and delightfully refreshing. In Mexico it's regarded as an everyday drink with a tart, fruity flavour not dissimilar from blackcurrant or cranberry juice. You can buy bags of dried hibiscus online or in wholefood shops. Make a batch and keep a jug cooling in the fridge on a warm summer's day.

SERVES 4–6
PREP: 10 MINUTES, PLUS COOLING

30g (1¼oz/generous ½ cup) edible
   dried hibiscus flowers

1 litre (1¾ pints/4¼ cups) boiling water

150g (5oz/¾ cup) caster
   (superfine) sugar

Juice of 1 lime

Ice cubes, to serve

You will also need 4 tumblers

1. Place the hibiscus in a large jug and pour over the boiling water. Stir through the caster sugar and leave to sit at room temperature until cooled.

2. Fill the tumblers with ice cubes, then divide the lime juice among them and pour over the aqua fresca. Alternatively, keep the jug of agua fresca in the fridge for up to 48 hours and enjoy over ice whenever you fancy.

GREEN AGUA FRESCA

A glass full of this refreshing drink can pack a punch on an early morning or as a mid-afternoon boost. The green agua fresca is a mix of fresh mint, citrusy lime and sweet kiwi fruit. Make a batch just for yourself or pour into a jug over ice to share at the table.

SERVES 4
PREP: 10 MINUTES

Leaves of ½ small bunch of mint

Zest and juice of 1 lime

5 small ripe kiwi fruit, peeled and
   roughly chopped

½ cucumber, deseeded and
   roughly chopped

2–3 tbsp agave syrup or runny honey

400ml (14fl oz/1⅔ cups) cold water

Ice cubes, to serve

You will also need 4 small glasses

1. Place the mint and lime zest and juice into a blender, along with the kiwi fruit, cucumber and agave syrup or honey, and pour in the water. Blitz until completely smooth.

2. Fill the glasses with ice and pour over the agua fresca.

PAPAYA, LIME AND CHILLI AGUA FRESCA

Papayas are those large, dark green, pear-shaped fruits you may see lingering in the tropical-fruit section of your local supermarket or greengrocer. Cracked open, the flesh is bright orange and perfectly sweet. They work beautifully whizzed up with lime as a delicious drink.

SERVES 4
PREP: 10 MINUTES

350g (12oz) ripe papayas, peeled, deseeded and roughly chopped

Zest and juice of 1 large lime

3 tbsp agave syrup or runny honey

500ml (18fl oz/2 cups) cold water

1 tsp chilli flakes

Ice cubes, to serve

You will also need 4 small glasses

1. Place the papayas, lime zest and juice and agave syrup or honey into a blender, add the water and blitz until smooth.

2. Fill the glasses with ice, divide the agua fresca mixture among them and add a pinch of chilli flakes to each one to serve.

LICUADOS

A licuado is a sweetened Mexican milkshake made with whole milk and fresh fruit. Refreshing and creamy, licuados can be made to order on the streets of Mexico City. This version is made with coconut, raspberry and sweet condensed milk, but you can mix and match the flavours. Try using different seasonal fruits or a shot of espresso coffee for an early-morning pick-me-up!

SERVES 2–4
PREP: 10 MINUTES

600ml (1 pint/2½ cups) whole milk

200ml (7fl oz/¾ cup) canned
    coconut milk

4 tbsp condensed milk

200g (7oz/1⅔ cups) fresh raspberries,
    plus extra to serve

Zest and juice of 2–3 limes, plus extra
    zest to serve

50g (2oz/1 cup) coconut flakes

You will also need 2 tall or 4 small glasses

1. Place the milk, coconut milk and condensed milk in a blender, along with the raspberries, and blend until smooth and creamy. Add the zest and juice of 2 limes, adding more if you feel it needs it.

2. Lightly toast the coconut flakes in a small pan over a low heat for 3–4 minutes until lightly browned, then remove from the heat.

3. Pour the licuado into the glasses and top each with some toasted coconut flakes, some lime zest and a few extra raspberries.

MEXICAN HOT CHOCOLATE

This is a far cry from a sachet of instant cocoa powder. Rich and spicy, it is exactly what you need on a cold autumn evening in front of the telly or poured into a flask and taken out on Bonfire Night to share with friends.

SERVES 4
PREP: 10 MINUTES
COOK: 5 MINUTES

800ml (1 pint 8fl oz/3⅓ cups)
　whole milk

1½ tsp ground cinnamon

¼ tsp cayenne pepper

5 tbsp (soft light) brown sugar

A pinch of freshly grated nutmeg, plus
　extra to serve

100g (3½ oz) dark chocolate (minimum
　80 per cent cocoa solids),
　finely chopped

A pinch of salt

FOR THE TOPPING

150ml (5fl oz/⅔ cup) double
　(heavy) cream

1 tbsp icing (confectioners') sugar

1 tsp árbol chilli flakes or standard
　chilli flakes

You will also need 4 medium-sized mugs

1. Pour the milk into a saucepan set over a low-medium heat and add the cinnamon, cayenne pepper, sugar and nutmeg. Whisk everything together and bring to a simmer.

2. Once the milk is steaming (don't let it boil), whisk through the dark chocolate until melted. Add the pinch of salt and keep warm over a low heat.

3. In a bowl, whisk together the double cream and icing sugar until soft and lightly whipped.

4. Pour the hot chocolate into the mugs and top with a spoonful of whipped cream, an extra grating of nutmeg and a generous pinch of warming chilli flakes.

INDEX

A

agave nectar/syrup 9
    classic margarita 124
    frozen watermelon and
        strawberry margarita 127
agua de Jamaica 131
aioli: chipotle aioli 107
    easy-peasy aioli 107
    pickled jalapeño aioli 107
    roasted garlic aioli 107
    zesty lime aioli 107
ancho chillies 9
    ancho smoked tofu and
        mango tacos 22
    skillet smoky ancho
        meatball nachos 60
apricots: charred fruit with
    pomegranate and vanilla
    mascarpone 121
    summer apricot and mint
    margarita 125
aqua frescas 131
    agua de Jamaica 131
    green aqua fresca 132
    papaya, lime and chilli agua
        fresca 133
avocado oil 9
guacamole 102
avocados: avocado crema 25
    avocado, popped black bean
        and radish tostadas 71
    crab and avocado tacos 26
    guacamole 102
    huevos rancheros 20

B

bacon: breakfast tacos 18
Baja fish tacos 28
barbecue jackfruit and rainbow
    slaw nachos 50

bavette steak: carne asada tacos
    38
beans 9
    avocado, popped black bean
        and radish tostadas 71
    black bean and fontina
        cheese quesadilla 84
black bean, charred corn and
    avocado crema tacos 25
    chicken and chipotle aioli
        tortas 78
    huevos rancheros 20
    nacho brunch bowls 46
    thrifty tacos with canned
        pineapple salsa 17
    ultimate classic nachos 44
    veggie chilli with chipotles
        in adobo 52
beef: carne asada tacos 38
    slow-cooked short rib
        nachos 51
    spicy beef burrito bites 79
biscuits: dark chocolate, rye and
    chilli cookies 116
black beans 9
    avocado, popped black bean
        and radish tostadas 71
    black bean and fontina
        cheese quesadilla 84
    black bean, charred corn and
        avocado crema tacos 25
    huevos rancheros 20
    ultimate classic nachos 44
black-eyed beans: veggie chilli
    with chipotles in adobo
    52
blistered-and-charred-chilli
    salsa 99
Bloody Mary 130
breakfast tacos 18

brunch bowls 46
burritos: spicy beef burrito bites
    79
butter: chilli and lime butter 74
butterbeans: nacho brunch
    bowls 46
buttermilk 12
    buttermilk fried chicken and
        pickled jalapeño aioli
        tacos 34
butternut squash: spiced squash,
    feta and mint chermoula
    tacos 24

C

cakes: tres leches cake 114
caramel: salted caramel sauce
    110
carne asada tacos 38
carnitas: pork carnitas with
    pineapple salsa 36
cashews: vegan sweet potato
    nachos with crispy onions
    56
ceviche 66
chard, Taleggio and chorizo
    empanadas 80
Cheddar: croque-monsieur
    quesadilla 86
    slow-cooked short rib
        nachos 51
    spiced mango chutney and
        chilli cheese nachos 48
    thrifty tacos with canned
        pineapple salsa 17
    ultimate classic nachos 44
cheese 12
    black bean and fontina
        cheese quesadilla 84
    breakfast tacos 18

brown-sugar roasted pineapple mini cheesecakes 120
chard, Taleggio and chorizo empanadas 80
charred fruit with pomegranate and vanilla mascarpone 121
charred spring onion cream cheese 88
charred spring onion and marinated feta tacos 21
charred vegetable and ricotta nachos 54
croque-monsieur quesadilla 86
Greek nachos with tomato and cucumber salsa 58
mushroom, charred spring onion and blue cheese quesadilla 87
skillet smoky ancho meatball nachos 60
slow-cooked short rib nachos 51
spiced mango chutney and chilli cheese nachos 48
spiced squash, feta and mint chermoula tacos 24
thrifty tacos with canned pineapple salsa 17
ultimate classic nachos 44
cheesecakes: brown-sugar roasted pineapple mini cheesecakes 120
chermoula: spiced squash, feta and mint chermoula tacos 24
chicken: buttermilk fried chicken and pickled jalapeño aioli tacos 34
chicken and chipotle aioli tortas 78
fiery habanero chicken wings 82
smoky crispy chicken and charred corn nachos 62

chile de árbol 9
chilli: veggie chilli with chipotles in adobo 52
chilli flakes 10
chilli and lime butter 74
dark chocolate, rye and chilli cookies 116
papaya, lime and chilli agua fresca 133
chilli powder 10
chilli sauce see Cholula chilli sauce
chillies: dried chillies 9
fresh chillies 12
blistered-and-charred-chilli salsa 99
easy pickled jalapeños 106
fiery habanero chilli sauce 101
pickled jalapeño aioli 107
see also ancho chillies; chipotle chillies; habanero chillies; jalapeño chillies
chipotles in adobo 10
veggie chilli with chipotles in adobo 52
chipotle aioli 107
chicken and chipotle aioli tortas 78
crispy squid and sunshine salad tacos 30
chipotle chilli paste 10
chipotle aioli 107
smoky chipotle and tomato chutney 100
chipotle chillies 9
chocolate: chocolate sauce 110
dark chocolate, rye and chilli cookies 116
hot chocolate 136
Cholula chilli sauce 10
Cholula Marie Rose sauce 90
Mexicana Bloody Mary 130
nacho brunch bowls 46

chorizo: blistered chorizo and potato tacos 33
chard, Taleggio and chorizo empanadas 80
chorizo and prawn topped nachos 65
nacho brunch bowls 46
churros 110
churros ice-cream sandwiches 112–13
chutney: smoky chipotle and tomato chutney 100
cinnamon ice cream 113
coconut: licuados 134
cod: Baja fish tacos 28
Cointreau: classic margarita 124
Comté: croque-monsieur quesadilla 86
cookies: dark chocolate, rye and chilli cookies 116
corn on the cob: black bean, charred corn and avocado crema tacos 25
grilled corn on the cob with chilli and lime butter 74
smoky crispy chicken and charred corn nachos 62
corn tortillas 10, 12
homemade soft corn tortillas 16
cornbread with charred spring onion cream cheese 88
cornmeal 10
crab and avocado tacos 26
cream cheese: brown-sugar roasted pineapple mini cheesecakes 120
charred spring onion cream cheese 88
crema 12, 82
croque-monsieur quesadilla 86
cucumbers: pickled cucumber 32
tomato and cucumber salsa 58

E
eggs: breakfast tacos 18

huevos rancheros 20
nacho brunch bowls 46
zesty lime aioli 107
empanadas: chard, Taleggio and
    chorizo empanadas 80

F

feta: charred spring onion and
    marinated feta tacos 21
    Greek nachos with tomato
        and cucumber salsa 58
    spiced squash, feta and mint
        chermoula tacos 24
fiery habanero chicken wings
    82
fiery habanero chilli sauce 101
fish: Baja fish tacos 28
    ceviche 66
    fish finger tacos with quick
        pickled cucumber 32
    smoked salmon and spring
        onion tostadas 72
    tuna and sesame tostadas 70
    see also seafood
fontina cheese: black bean and
    fontina cheese quesadilla 84
    skillet smoky ancho
        meatball nachos 60

G

garlic: roasted garlic aioli 107
Gouda: thrifty tacos with
    canned pineapple salsa 17
Greek nachos with tomato and
    cucumber salsa 58
green aqua fresca 132
green sauce 38
green tomatillo salsa 98
guacamole 102

H

habanero chillies 9
    fiery habanero chicken
        wings 82
    fiery habanero chilli sauce
        101
haddock: fish finger tacos with
    quick pickled cucumber 32

halloumi: breakfast tacos 18
hibiscus flowers 10
    hibiscus agua fresca 131
    hibiscus ripple ice lollies
        118
hot chocolate 136
huevos rancheros 20

I

ice cream: cinnamon ice cream
    113
    ice-cream sandwiches
        112–13
ice lollies: hibiscus ripple ice
    lollies 118

J

jackfruit and rainbow slaw
    nachos 50
jalapeño chillies 10, 12
    buttermilk fried chicken and
        pickled jalapeño aioli
        tacos 34
    easy pickled jalapeños 106
    pickled jalapeño aioli 107

K

kidney beans: veggie chilli with
    chipotles in adobo 52
kiwi fruit: green aqua fresca
    132

L

lamb: Middle Eastern lamb
    nachos 64
licuados 134
limes: chilli and lime butter 74
    classic margarita 124
    frozen watermelon and
        strawberry margarita
        127
    green aqua fresca 132
    papaya, lime and chilli agua
        fresca 133
    rhubarb and vanilla
        margarita 126
    summer apricot and mint
        margarita 125

watermelon wedges
    with lime and pink
        peppercorn salt 76
zesty lime aioli 107

M

mango chutney: spiced mango
    chutney and chilli cheese
        nachos 48
mangoes: ancho smoked tofu
    and mango tacos 22
margaritas: classic margarita
    124
    frozen watermelon and
        strawberry margarita 127
    rhubarb and vanilla
        margarita 126
    summer apricot and mint
        margarita 125
Marie Rose sauce 90
masa harina flour 10
    homemade soft corn
        tortillas 16
mascarpone: charred fruit with
    pomegranate and vanilla
        mascarpone 121
meatballs: skillet smoky ancho
    meatball nachos 60
Middle Eastern lamb nachos 64
milkshakes 134
mint: green aqua fresca 132
    spiced squash, feta and mint
        chermoula tacos 24
    summer apricot and mint
        margarita 125
mozzarella: spiced mango
    chutney and chilli cheese
        nachos 48
    ultimate classic nachos 44
mushrooms: mushroom, charred
    spring onion and blue
        cheese quesadilla 87
    nacho brunch bowls 46

N

nachos 13
    barbecue jackfruit and
        rainbow slaw nachos 50

ceviche 66
charred vegetable and
    ricotta nachos 54
chorizo and prawn topped
    nachos 65
deep-fried tortilla chips 42
easy baked tortilla chips 43
Greek nachos with tomato
    and cucumber salsa 58
Middle Eastern lamb
    nachos 64
nacho brunch bowls 46
skillet smoky ancho
    meatball nachos 60
slow-cooked short rib
    nachos 51
smoky crispy chicken and
    charred corn nachos 62
spiced mango chutney and
    chilli cheese nachos 48
ultimate classic nachos 44
vegan sweet potato nachos
    with crispy onions 56
veggie chilli with chipotles
    in adobo 52
nuts: Mexican spiced nuts and
    seeds 75

O
onions 12
    pink pickled onions 104
    vegan sweet potato nachos
        with crispy onions 56
    see also spring onions
oranges: crispy squid and
    sunshine salad tacos 30
oregano 10

P
papaya, lime and chilli agua
    fresca 133
pastry: chard, Taleggio and
    chorizo empanadas 80
peaches: charred fruit with
    pomegranate and vanilla
    mascarpone 121
peppers: charred vegetable and
    ricotta nachos 54

veggie chilli with chipotles
    in adobo 52
pickled jalapeño aioli 107
    buttermilk fried chicken and
        pickled jalapeño aioli
        tacos 34
pickles: easy pickled jalapeños 106
    pickled cucumber 32
    pink pickled onions 104
    smoky chipotle and tomato
        chutney 100
pico de gallo salsa 95
pineapple: brown-sugar roasted
    pineapple mini cheesecakes
    120
    canned pineapple salsa 17
    pineapple salsa 36
pink peppercorns: watermelon
    wedges with lime and pink
    peppercorn salt 76
pink pickled onions 104
pinto beans: huevos rancheros
    20
polenta 10
    cornbread with charred
        spring onion cream
        cheese 88
pomegranate seeds 30
    charred fruit with
        pomegranate and vanilla
        mascarpone 121
pork: pork carnitas with
    pineapple salsa 36
    skillet smoky ancho
        meatball nachos 60
potatoes: blistered chorizo and
    potato tacos 33
prawns: chorizo and prawn
    topped nachos 65
    pint of prawns with Cholula
        Marie Rose 90
pumpkin seeds: Mexican spiced
    nuts and seeds 75

Q
quesadillas 84
    black bean and fontina
        cheese quesadilla 84

croque-monsieur quesadilla
    86
    mushroom, charred spring
        onion and blue cheese
        quesadilla 87
queso fresco 12

R
radishes: avocado, popped black
    bean and radish tostadas 71
rainbow slaw 50
raspberries: hibiscus ripple ice
    lollies 118
    licuados 134
refried beans 9
    chicken and chipotle aioli
        tortas 78
rhubarb and vanilla margarita
    126
ribs: slow-cooked short rib
    nachos 51
ricotta: charred vegetable and
    ricotta nachos 54
rye: dark chocolate, rye and
    chilli cookies 116

S
salmon: smoked salmon and
    spring onion tostadas 72
salsas: blistered-and-charred-
    chilli salsa 99
    canned pineapple salsa 17
    green tomatillo salsa 98
    mango salsa 22
    pico de gallo salsa 95
    pineapple salsa 36
    tomato and cucumber salsa
        58
    vine-ripened tomato salsa
        94
salted caramel sauce 110
sauces: chocolate sauce 110
    Cholula Marie Rose sauce
        90
    fiery habanero chilli sauce
        101
    green sauce 38
    salted caramel sauce 110

sea bass: ceviche 66
seafood: chorizo and prawn
    topped nachos 65
    crab and avocado tacos 26
    crispy squid and sunshine
        salad tacos 30
    pint of prawns with Cholula
        Marie Rose 90
sesame: tuna and sesame
    tostadas 70
slaw: rainbow slaw 50
soured cream 12
    crema 82
spinach: breakfast tacos 18
spring onions: charred spring
    onion and marinated feta
    tacos 21
    mushroom, charred spring
        onion and blue cheese
        quesadilla 87
    smoked salmon and spring
        onion tostadas 72
squash: spiced squash, feta and
    mint chermoula tacos 24
squid: crispy squid and sunshine
    salad tacos 30
steak: carne asada tacos 38
strawberries: frozen watermelon
    and strawberry margarita 127
sunshine salad 30
sweet potato nachos with crispy
    onions 56

T
tacos 13
    ancho smoked tofu and
        mango tacos 22
    Baja fish tacos 28
    black bean, charred corn and
        avocado crema tacos
        25
    blistered chorizo and potato
        tacos 33
    breakfast tacos 18
    buttermilk fried chicken and
        pickled jalapeño aioli
        tacos 34
    carne asada tacos 38

charred spring onion and
    marinated feta tacos 21
crab and avocado tacos 26
crispy squid and sunshine
    salad tacos 30
fish finger tacos with quick
    pickled cucumber 32
homemade soft corn
    tortillas 16
huevos rancheros 20
pork carnitas with pineapple
    salsa 36
spiced squash, feta and mint
    chermoula tacos 24
thrifty tacos with canned
    pineapple salsa 17
Taleggio: chard, Taleggio and
    chorizo empanadas 80
    slow-cooked short rib
        nachos 51
tequila: classic margarita 124
    frozen watermelon and
        strawberry margarita
        127
    rhubarb and vanilla
        margarita 126
    summer apricot and mint
        margarita 125
tofu: ancho smoked tofu
    and mango tacos 22
tomatillos 9
    green tomatillo salsa 98
tomatoes: blistered-and-
    charred-chilli salsa 99
    breakfast tacos 18
    charred vegetable and
        ricotta nachos 54
    fiery habanero chilli sauce
        101
    pico de gallo salsa 95
    smoky chipotle and tomato
        chutney 100
    thrifty tacos with canned
        pineapple salsa 17
    tomato and cucumber salsa
        58
    vine-ripened tomato salsa
        94

tortas: chicken and chipotle aioli
    tortas 78
tortilla chips 12
    deep-fried tortilla chips 42
    easy baked tortilla chips 43
    see also nachos
tortillas 10, 12
    homemade soft corn
        tortillas 16
    see also burritos; quesadillas;
        tacos; tostadas
tostadas 70
    avocado, popped black bean
        and radish tostadas 71
    smoked salmon and spring
        onion tostadas 72
    tuna and sesame tostadas
        70
tres leches cake 114
triple sec: classic margarita 124
tuna and sesame tostadas 70

V
vanilla: charred fruit with
    pomegranate and vanilla
    mascarpone 121
    rhubarb and vanilla
        margarita 126
vegan sweet potato nachos with
    crispy onions 56
veggie chilli with chipotles in
    adobo 52
    vodka: Mexicana Bloody
        Mary 130

W
watermelon: frozen watermelon
    and strawberry margarita
    127
    watermelon wedges
        with lime and pink
        peppercorn salt 76

ACKNOWLEDGEMENTS

I'm so lucky to be surrounded by positivity and support regarding my lovely job, if you can call this a job!

Firstly, I want to thank my dreamy group of friends who always encourage me to cook, write and feed them. From my guy pals back in Brighton to best friends in Edinburgh and my friends in London, thank you all for your unwavering support. To those who I went to cookery school with, I'm so lucky to have found people that understand how important food is in life; you all know who you are.

Thanks also to Zanna and Nathan who lived with me over the months of flipping tacos, stuffing empanadas into their mouths and smearing guacamole round our little east London kitchen. Thanks for always being so great and making me laugh so much.

A huge thank you to Lydia Good who gave me the opportunity to write this fun book! And also to James, Georgina and the amazing team at HarperCollins who have worked so hard. You've always been so chilled about everything and enthusiastic about my ideas, so thanks so much. To lovely Faith Mason who shot the photographs in this book, ever the perfectionist and now someone who I call a firm friend. Thank you to Alex for the props; you put together my vision, what more can you ask for? Thanks to my mates Nicola and Katie for our week of shooting together on the hottest spring week ever recorded! You're both too much fun in the kitchen.

A special thank you to my friend and fellow writer Rosie Reynolds who champions everything I do. You taught me that food is about being true to yourself; it can be fun, tacky, nostalgic and messy but still bloomin' beautiful!

Finally, I want to thank my little family. My sisters who are always excited about my cooking and general life in London and always have been. But most of all my lovely mum and dad who, for as long as I can remember, have let me feel my way through life without any pressure. They have always encouraged me to do exactly what I want in life, and have shown me support that is unwavering. It began many years before they sent me off to London to cookery school. I'll never be able to thank you both enough.

HarperCollins*Publishers*
1 London Bridge Street
London SE1 9GF

www.harpercollins.co.uk

First published by HarperCollins*Publishers* 2018

1 3 5 7 9 10 8 6 4 2

© HarperCollins*Publishers* 2018

Photographer: Faith Mason
Food Stylist: Esther Clark
Prop Stylist: Alexander Breeze

A catalogue record of this book is available from the British Library

HB ISBN 978-0-00-830129-3
EB ISBN 978-0-00-830160-6

Printed and bound in Latvia

MIX
Paper from
responsible sources
FSC **FSC™ C007454**
www.fsc.org

FSC™ is a non-profit international organisation established to promote the
responsible management of the world's forests. Products carrying the FSC
label are independently certified to assure consumers that they come from
forests that are managed to meet the social, economic and ecological needs
of present and future generations, and other controlled sources.

Find out more about HarperCollins and the environment at
www.harpercollins.co.uk/green